A Bowyer Book
Published in the United Kingdom
by Bowyer Publishing in 2018
Copyright © Dave Fanning
All rights reserved

Author's Web Address: http://philthefireengine.com

The moral right of the author has been asserted.

No part of this book may be reproduced, stored in a retrieval system, or transmitted in any form or by any means without the prior written consent of the publisher, nor reproduced, circulated in any manner in any form or binding other than that in which it is published and without a similar condition including this condition being imposed on the subsequent purchaser. The only exception is a reviewer who may publish short excerpts in a published review. Commercialised book summaries are expressly prohibited and unauthorised unless specifically licensed by the publisher.

This book is presented for information and entertainment purposes only. The information presented herein represents the view of the author at date of publication. The author reserves the right to alter and update opinions based on new information and new conditions.

While every attempt has been made to verify the information in this book, neither the author nor affiliates/partners assume any responsibility for errors, inaccuracies, or omissions. At no time can any of the information herein be construed as professional, investment, tax, accounting, or legal advice, nor does it constitute a recommendation or warrant of suitability for any particular business, industry, transaction, or business strategy.

ISBN 978-1-9996273-7-9
Book Design by Tiger Ink, Hampshire, England

Use of front cover photo courtesy of photographer Alan Kennett
Use of black and white photos and colour photo on back cover courtesy of The Liverpool Echo

Bowyer Publishing
A Division of Archer Business Group
Unit F, Meadow View Business Park
Winchester Road, Hampshire SO32 1HJ
England

Fanning the Flames

FANNING THE FLAMES

Recollections of a lost era of firefighting

Dave Fanning

CONTENTS

FANNING THE FLAMES...iii
FOREWORD 1
INTRODUCTION 2
   Flashback 2
   The power of story telling 3
CHAPTER ONE.. 6
   Hard lessons in early training................................... 6
   give later strength 6
   Clarifying instructions and self confidence 13
   My first experience of death. 17
   Of snoring and practical jokes 18
   Airport duties – not all fire related........................ 20
   The airport rescue boat.. 22
   An unexpected canine hazard 23
CHAPTER TWO 25
   Massive tyre blaze 25
   Keep Clear 26
   To be a fire engine driver 28
   Learning from the experience of others............... 29
   Is all clear? 30
CHAPTER THREE 34
   The power of silence for critical focus 34
   The ring of pain... 35
   Manning the boat.. 36
   Barn haunting 38
   Tough and realistic national training 41
   Promotion 44
CHAPTER FOUR.. 49
   The Firefighter Strike... 49

Temporary Station Officer Posting 50
Airport Fire Officer's Training 51
My own watch at last 52
Fire in Ritson Street 54
Upper Parliament Street chip fire and arson 58

CHAPTER FIVE 60

Explosions and smoke inhalation 60
A blood bath 65

CHAPTER SIX 69

The gas fire explosion 69
Crew bravery and commendations 72
Arson and fires set accidentally by children 73
The birth of Phil the Fire Engine 79
A case of mistaken identity 81
Rubber tyres ablaze 82
Local house fire with two survivors 83
Not just fighting fires 84

CHAPTER EIGHT 91

Introducing the fire station to the locals 91
Unusual fire engine freight 92
Helping the ladies 93
Slow path to promotion 95
Unfair mantle of authority on a young officer 96

CHAPTER NINE 98

Firefighting in civil unrest 98
How to grow £250 to £700 99
Rank doesn't always deserve respect 101
Finally a proper promotion –temporarily 103

CHAPTER TEN 107

Changes of direction 107
Time to form a plan. 110

Earning money for the Fire Service 111
A derelict bus has an unexpected end... 113
CHAPTER ELEVEN 115
Firefighting training for refugee ships... 115
Creating a 'boil over' 120
Back to the beginning 120
CHAPTER TWELVE.. 122
Station Commander Duties 122
Initiating a community solution 124
Royal recognition 127
CHAPTER THIRTEEN.. 133
The need for fire station security 133
Honouring former firefighters.. 135
Issues of life and death not related to fire fighting........................ 138
CHAPTER FOURTEEN 144
The blonde on a ledge in her negligée 144
Firefighting among drug use remains 146
A rush construction job gone wrong... 148
Fire arms at the incident scene 150
CHAPTER FIFTEEN 153
Training in fighting ship fires 153
CHAPTER SIXTEEN 162
Outreach to young people in the community 162
More strike action 163
Cotton candy on fire.. 164
Avoidable domestic fires.. 166
Firefighters' Attitude Improvement Meeting 166
Drawing the final line 169

FOREWORD

These are the stories of a legacy of firefighting in Liverpool, England, in an era that had challenges of the sort no longer faced by firefighters today.

This was a time when more than 700 ships a week offloaded their often highly volatile cargoes in the docks of the River Mersey.

It was a time when firefighters had to master the use of the hook and ladder to enter buildings ablaze, and when little regard for Health and Safety saw them wearing what were no more than the equivalent of gardening gloves as they undertook their duties.

It is in this context that Dave Fanning brings us his memories of leading firefighting on Merseyside.

Poignant, funny, and full of down-to-earth detail and valuable lessons for any leader of people, these stories bring to life the Liverpool of the 1970s, 80s and early 90s, with humour and insight typical of the people on Merseyside.

INTRODUCTION

Flashback

I was lying at the head of the staircase, eyes stinging, nose running, the smoke was getting thicker. What was taking them so long? The baby was in that room. When we arrived, the mother had screamed to me that her child was in the back bedroom.

I could hear the four firefighters in the bedroom. There was a sudden loud crash as the cold water from the hose jet hit the window and it shattered, then a muffled shout and the sound of someone running towards me. I moved backwards down the stairs on my stomach, reached the bottom, and stood up. Through the smoke a firefighter appeared carrying a bundle that contained the baby.

"The ambulance is outside" I shouted. As he passed me with the child I saw it was too late. The baby was dead on arrival at the hospital.

I had progressed through the ranks and was in charge of one of the busiest one-pump fire stations in the country, possibly Europe, but today I felt failure, despair and defeat.

We had a proud boast on Blue Watch at Toxteth. At every fire we had attended to date, if someone was trapped and alive when we arrived, we had saved them: but not today. I felt numb. My son John had been born just six months ago. What if that had been my child?

The guys looked shell shocked. As usual when we returned to the station not a lot was said; we all kept our thoughts to ourselves. Mine returned to why I had become a firefighter. Despite the heartbreak of incidents like this, my chosen profession remained my passion.

The power of story telling

I had always wanted to be a firefighter from an early age thanks to my 'Uncle George'.

'Uncle' George Kiffin was some distant relative on my mother's side of the family and had served in the Auxiliary Fire Service during the Second World War.

At Christmas and New Year – when there were large gatherings of family and friends in a large terraced house in Shaw Street Liverpool and when drinks had been flowing – George would be asked about the Blitz and what he had seen and done during that terrible time. To put this into context, the German *Luftwaffe* had targeted Liverpool as a key city to destroy.

Liverpool was the largest port on the west coast of the country and had long been the destination of trans-Atlantic crossings. It was the key maritime link to North America. The 18 km *(11 miles)* of ports, quays and docks handled over 90% of all the war material that arrived from abroad to sustain our island nation during the Second World War.

Expecting the ports to be a target, in 1939 the government implemented 'Operation Pied Piper'. This evacuated over 8,500 children, parents and teachers to Wales, Cheshire, Shrewsbury and Shropshire.

However, when the predicted bombing didn't happen, many parents brought their children home. Sadly, when the Blitz began, with 160 bombers attacking on 28th August 1940, over 40% of the evacuees were back in the city.

In November of that year an Air Raid Shelter in Liverpool was hit – killing 160 people. Churchill proclaimed it the "single worst incident of the war".

Bombing continued in Liverpool, with a sustained period from 20-22 December 1940.

In the New Year the bombing was less intense until May, when a seven-night bombardment devastated much of the city.

Between May 1st and 7th, 681 bombers shed their loads over the city: 2,315 highly explosive bombs and other types that included fire-bombs. The bombing incapacitated 144 of the cargo berths.

On the 3rd May the *SS Malakand* was hit. Firemen managed to put the blaze on the ship out, but the flames had spread to sheds that had already been demolished by previous bombing raids and it was impossible to extinguish the intense blaze that erupted. The flames from the sheds then returned to engulf the ship.

Despite valiant firefighting efforts over 1,000 bombs in the cargo hold exploded, destroying one of the docks and its surrounding quays. The strength of the explosion deposited pieces of ship hull in a park 1.6km *(1 mile)* away. The fire burnt for three days before extinguishing itself for lack of anything else to burn.

Post-war German reports stated that Liverpool sustained the most intense attack of any location in Britain.

Although about 4,000 people died from the bombing of Liverpool and its environs, the government wanted to keep reporting of the extent of damage to the docks to a minimum.

Even years after the war, most of the country had no idea that the city had suffered so greatly.

On the 3rd and 4th of May alone, Liverpool firefighters attended over 400 fires.

As a small boy I listened intently as George recalled the many blazes he fought as the Nazis carried out their constant bombing of Liverpool, trying to cut off the country's supply line through the port.

He told of then having to leave Liverpool and move on to other cities such as Coventry and Portsmouth to use his hard-honed skills and experience to supplement local fire fighting forces as the Nazis chose different targets to blitz.

These tales included vivid reminiscences of buildings collapsing, colleagues disappearing when floors gave way - never to be seen again: of lives saved and many lives lost.

Listening intently as Uncle George sat by the large open fireplace holding everyone's attention, I decided there and then I wanted to fight fires.

I wanted to save lives and, just like him, to serve the public.

CHAPTER ONE

Hard lessons in early training

give later strength

My career had begun in August 1964, at 16 years of age. I was the very first junior fireman appointed by Liverpool Brigade when they started a Cadet Firefighter scheme.

There were 9 of us on that very first course. My service number was 7001.

The Junior Fireman Scheme was designed to give young men a chance to join the fire service when they reached the age of 18. Until that time, we attended college on a Thursday and Friday to continue with our education.

On Monday, Tuesday, and Wednesday we had a rigorous schedule of ladder drills and hose drills; and we learnt about hydraulics and all the other myriad technical and points of strategy that we needed to know for a career in the fire brigade.

Over the next two years for 9 weeks at a time the young men on the course were split into three groups. Those groups remained together for the period and spent time in every department in the fire brigade. This gave each cadet a good grounding in how all the different parts worked together to provide an efficient service to the people of Liverpool.

On Saturday mornings we had to report to the training school at Banks Road in Garston, very close to Liverpool Airport. Here we learnt squad drill, how to wash hose, and to clean the training school building.

Squad drill was hilarious. We couldn't start off with our left foot. We swung our arms at different times to our feet and when we had to change direction or make an 'about turn' manoeuvre, someone would crash into someone else, or trip and fall over.

Our instructors were all ex-army or navy personnel. They seemed to take great delight in shouting very loudly. I remember that they went bright red in the face when they were three inches away from your nose if you were responsible for going in the wrong direction from everyone else on the drill ground, or were unfortunate enough to end up on the concrete having tripped over someone's foot.

When we were not attending college, we practised all day. As we gained more experience we thankfully were better able to execute all of the different drills, not just squad drill. I never felt we learnt much from the squad drill but certainly after two years of practice we were a firmly bonded group.

One of the training sessions that I will always remember was Hook Ladder Drill.

Hook ladders were metal ladders about four and a half metres *(about 14.7 feet)* in length. The top of the ladder had a large metal hook, with teeth cut underneath.

In theory, the hook ladder enabled you to climb up the outside of a building by using only one ladder. It went like this:
- From the ground floor you would smash a window on the first floor, pull the hook down onto the windowsill inside the building. The teeth would bite into the wood to secure the ladder.
- You then would climb up to the first floor, enter it, and then smash the hook through a second-floor window, and so on until you reached the required floor.

Today, it would be a Health and Safety nightmare.

Anyway, at some time, each of us had the task of climbing up the drill tower at Banks Road and onto the roof, using a single hook ladder. It was a very frightening experience and took four or five practice runs to finally scramble onto the tower roof.

The secret of ensuring that the ladder hook cut into the wooden window ledge securely was to lean your body weight away from the ladder.

This was far easier said than done, as the instinct of self-preservation tells you the exact opposite: to hang on for grim death and keep your body as close to the ladder as you possibly can.

Quite often the instructor would shout out: "Don't shag the ladder boy, stick your arse out. Keep your arms straight. You'll find it easier that way."

One of the squad had to perform the hook ladder drill during the Passing Out Parade, in front of the Chief Fire Officer and the Lord Mayor. No one volunteered.

At one of the last practice sessions the 'lucky man' chosen to perform on the big day was going through his paces. He reached the floor below the roof level and lifted the ladder to hook onto the very final windowsill. This was about 20 metres *(almost 66 feet)* or more above the concrete yard. He then pulled down on the ladder to make sure it gripped onto the wooden surface; leant out correctly; put his left foot on the ladder; and swung out into space to begin the final climb.

What no one had realised on the day was that the door onto the roof from the drill tower internal staircase had blown open in the wind, so instead of the ladder hooking onto the sill, it hooked over the open door.

This left our lucky 'volunteer' swinging on the ladder 18 metres *(60 feet)* above the ground - like the pendulum on a clock.

As we all stood transfixed, watching our colleague swinging above us, the drill instructor ran into the tower, climbed the internal metal ladder incredibly fast, and upon reaching the swinging ladder, grabbed the fireman and pulled him into the tower safely.

To our undying admiration, when the 'lucky man' returned to terra firma, he promptly volunteered to go back up. He completed the climb: this time without a hitch.

Though the training seemed to go on all day, every day, it was good education for our future years in the fire service.

Unbeknown to us, some of the older firemen at the time thought that this new programme was designed so that we would be promoted very quickly to officers. They drew an implication that long-serving officers may be passed over in our favour.

Management was probably unaware of this – and had not anticipated that such a thought might result from implementing a new scheme with no appropriate briefing. In the absence of management of this expectation, there was some resentment on a number of stations where we had to gain experience. This resulted in us being either completely ignored, or given menial tasks to complete during our seven-week assignment to that station.

The seven weeks I enjoyed most were those in the control room. This was where you could gauge the activity in the day-to-day running of Liverpool Fire Brigade.

We were allowed to answer 999 calls *(the British Emergency number)* with one of the control staff listening in to supervise, and eventually we were allowed to 'turn the stations out' by making announcements over the loudspeaker system.

The first station I turned out was Hatton Garden, which at the time was Brigade Headquarters. I cannot remember the address of the call, but I do remember shaking in case I gave out the wrong information.

This process of 'turning out' was explicit in its instructions:

- You had to press a button six times. The resulting sound was like pips – the sort of high-pitched, intermittent sound that announces the time on the radio or, in some countries, indicates that the telephone you are calling is busy. This sound alerted the station to an upcoming announcement.
- You then gave the station's identification number, and details of what appliances had to attend, followed by the address, which had to be repeated.

It was exciting when you were in the control room and a large number of appliances were turned out at a major incident.

Someone had to make a written note of all the appliances attending. They then had to check whether another station would have to provide cover for the equipment that had been sent out if the station concerned was designated as a Key Station, which was one that always had to have an appliance on location. Key stations were designated due to the perceived risk in that station area. That risk might be that the station area had many chemical factories or, because of population density it had a substantial 'life risk'.

Hatton Garden was a key station because it covered Liverpool City Centre: it had three fire engines, a turntable ladder, an emergency tender and a control van.

As soon as Hatton Garden's three fire engines turned out anywhere, another station had to stand in as cover.

At that time Liverpool Fire Brigade was made up of the following three divisions.

Central Division, with five stations:
C1 Hatton Garden: the city centre
C2 Belvidere Road: Toxteth
C3 Coburg Dock: the south dockland
C4 Canada Dock: for the north dockland
C5 Westminster Road: Scotland Road area.

Northern Division, with four stations:
N1 Longmoor Lane: Walton Hospital and the industrial estates
N2 Storrington Avenue: the newer housing estates in Croxteth
N3 Derby Lane: Old Swan
N4 Durning Road: Picton and Wavertree areas.

Southern Division, with four stations
S1 Mather Avenue: Allerton and Mossley Hill
S2 Belle Vale: the new housing estate of Netherley, plus Childwall, and Gateacre
S3 Conleach Road: the Speke area
S4 Banks Road: Garston and Liverpool Airport.

Finally, after two years of intensive training and having performed the required drill of the Passing Out Parade, the 9 recruits who had started back in 1964 stood at the training school waiting to hear to which station they were to be posted.

We all knew the busy stations as we had served on them during our two years travelling around the brigade. Each of us wanted to be posted to any one of them, so we could begin fighting fires for real.

My heart sank when I heard them call out my name and say S1 Mather Avenue was my first posting; not only mine, but two of my colleagues as well.

This was totally depressing. I wanted to fight fires, rescue damsels in distress, and feel like a hero, but Mather Avenue was known to be a quiet station – a 'grass station'. This was because, although it covered a large area, it was mostly modern housing and had very few industrial premises.

However, on the plus side, it was handy for home, as at that time I lived in Webster Road, scene of the infamous Cameo Murders in the 1950s.

Webster Road was less than a 15-minute walk to Mather Avenue.

The Cameo Cinema had been the site of a brutal double murder. The resulting indictment proved to be one of the greatest injustices in British legal history, with evidence either clearly tampered with, or not considered. In addition, later records indicated that there were clear indications of police coaching of witnesses.

Several years later the same Chief Superintendent of Police allegedly used similar methods to frame another two innocent parties in Manchester. Despite admission to the Criminal Cases Review Commission with new arguments and reportedly '11 bundles of previously undisclosed evidence', the case was rejected. An innocent man was convicted and executed.

Naturally, in light of this case, with one of the longest running criminal trials of history until then, everyone knew where I lived when I said 'Webster Road'.

It was an unusual way to make an entrance, but people certainly remembered me.

Clarifying instructions and self confidence

My first assignment at Mather Avenue in October 1966 was Night Duty. The station had two fire engines, a pump escape, and a pump, and in addition, an Emergency Tender. The pump escape had a large wooden ladder with wheels on. The ladder could reach to 15 metres. The pump carried a metal ladder that would reach to 9 metres *(almost 30 feet)*.

The Emergency Tender carried heavy cutting equipment, prolonged-use breathing apparatus, chemical protection suits, and lots of other specialised equipment.

To man the three machines, each tour of duty required:
- Five men for the pump escape
- Four men for the pump, and
- Six men for the emergency tender.

One man had to remain always on duty in the Watch Room to answer the phone and check the street fire alarm panel which was located there.

Liverpool used to have street fire alarms situated on most streets around the city. The fire alarm box was bright yellow and stood on top of a red post. If there was a house or factory fire in the street, anyone could smash the glass in the alarm and pull the handle. This would operate an alarm on the alarm panel on the station responsible for that street.

Two fire men were always assigned to the kitchen on nightshift, although only one of them also rode one of the appliances.

If all the machines turned out, the one left behind had to try and put all the plates with uneaten meals back into the hot plate oven and scribble the firefighter's name onto each plate with a marker pen – and remember who was sitting at what table.

In all, there were 20 men on each watch at the station when we arrived for our first tour of duty on Blue Watch. The night shift in those days was from 6pm to 9am the following day, and the shift patterns were unusual. In total you worked 56 hours per week, but in week two you worked 69 hours:

Week 1:
Monday & Tuesday: day shift.
Wednesday & Thursday: night shift.
Friday, Saturday & Sunday: off.
Week 2:
Monday & Tuesday: night.
Wednesday & Thursday: off.
Friday: day.
Saturday & Sunday: night
Week 3:
Monday &Tuesday: off.
Wednesday & Thursday: day
Friday: night
Saturday & Sunday: off.

In my first year at Mather Avenue I was paid £12 a week and at that time it would have taken me 15 years to reach the top fireman's wage.

My first boss on Blue Watch used to shout a lot. Not only when we were at fires but also while on the station – and he also swore heartily. At a fire there can be a time to shout, but continual shouting and swearing at the crew didn't help, and some guys resented the language being used. At the station, firefighters would try to stay out of the boss's way.

It took me many weeks to attend my first fire, but one morning just before we were going off night duty, we received a call to a house fire at a location about two minutes from the station.

When we arrived, there was a small fire inside the house. This was quickly dealt with.

The boss told me to go upstairs and open the windows to let the smoke out.

Up I went, coughing in the light smoke at the top of the stairs. I opened the windows in bedroom one and then made my way into the main bedroom. My eyes were stinging now with the smoke and I was coughing a little more.

I opened one big window but the other window was very stiff. Knowing that the boss would shout if I didn't open all the windows, I pushed harder. My hand slipped off the wooden frame and went straight through the glass.

The boss, thinking I had gone up stairs and was smashing every window with my fireman's axe, came up the stairs three at a time screaming: "What are you f****** doing, you stupid idiot? Get downstairs out of my sight."

I slid downstairs, totally embarrassed, and headed into the street before climbing into the back of the fire engine.

I noticed at this time that my hand was bleeding, but decided to lie low. When we got back to the station I crept into the station office and asked the Sub Officer if I could have a plaster. Just then the boss walked in.

"A f****** plaster? You did more damage than the fire, and you expect first aid?" He was enraged, and stormed out of the office.

The Sub Officer, who was more sympathetic, tended to my wound. I walked home feeling very miserable.

I vowed that if I became an officer I would be sympathetic in such circumstances. Here I was, not long out of the training school and it was my first experience turning out after weeks of waiting. There had been not a word of guidance or encouragement, and I was presumed to have done something I hadn't – all because the boss had his mind made up before he started shouting and before he had time to check his facts.

One night the boss's shouting upset someone too much. It was about 2.30 am when the station loudspeaker system spluttered into life and the lights came on in the night room. The pump escape was ordered to a house fire in our area.

When all the crew was on the machine, the boss asked if we had the address. To a man we all said that control had stated 'Elmar Road', so the driver shot off in the direction of Elmar Road.

When we entered Elmar Road it was a cul-de-sac with only a few houses.

The house number given by the caller was number 46 but the house numbers in Elmar Road only went up to 20.

Our boss called Control on the radio to check the address and was told that the correct address was 46 *Alma* Road, which was about a mile away from where we were.

The boss went into overdrive, shouting at the driver that he was a stupid so-and-so and had brought us to the wrong address.

To the boss's amazement, and to ours, the driver took the keys from the ignition, gave them to the boss and said: "Here drive it yourself. I am not being spoken to like that." He then left the cab and started to walk back to the fire station.

We all sat there with our mouths wide open as the boss leapt out of the cab and chased after the driver, apologising profusely and pleading with him to drive us to the correct address, which he eventually did.

We found a house under construction blazing away in the night sky.

It was an easy mistake to make. The road names sound very similar, but we all thought that Control had said 'Elmar Road' on the first call we received.

In the years to come as an officer, I would always confirm the address myself with the control room when I booked mobile to the incident. From the actions of the driver I also took the message of having respect for yourself at all times.

My first experience of death.

One sunny day in 1967 on dinner break, some of the lads were having a kick-about in the station yard, while the rest were soaking up the sun's rays.

It was in this relaxed context that a smartly dressed lady walked down the ramp at the rear of the station and asked the guys for help. She was locked out of her flat that was situated about 100 yards from the station. Her husband was supposed to be in, but she thought he must have forgotten that she was returning early from work.

The boss decided that as it was a lovely day we would take the escape ladder off the machine, push it up the concrete ramp and pitch it to the third floor flat window and enter to let this lady in.

We came up the ramp, pushing the ladder. One of the crew had walked to the nearby building with the lady to look at where we could safely put the ladder, just in case the ground was uneven. Then the lady noticed that her husband's car was in the garage. She feared that, as he wasn't answering, he may have been taken ill. I was sent back to get the oxygen set from the pump engine swiftly to the scene.

As I arrived at the block of apartments carrying the oxygen equipment, the boss was at the top of the ladder using a penknife to slide the window catch open. He shouted down to the crew to meet him outside the flat door. Together with the lady, we climbed the stairs to the top floor.

As we reached the flat entrance, the boss came out, grabbed me, and said: "Get the oxygen on him. He's in the kitchen."

At this point every one of us could smell gas. I ran in, and there was the lady's husband lying on the floor with his head in the gas oven. I heard the terrible screams from her as the rest of the crew stopped her from entering until the flat had been ventilated and there was no chance of the gas being ignited.

I put the oxygen mask on the casualty but he was obviously dead and had been like that for some time.

I was 19, and here I was with my first dead body. I had nightmares for a few nights afterwards. I kept waking after seeing the man's face in a dream.

In the years to come there would be many more dead bodies, and eventually they would become easier to deal with. It was different when it was a child.

I always felt that with adults they should have had the good sense not to smoke and fall asleep in bed, not to leave pans unattended on the stove or come home drunk and drop a cigarette on the sofa. But children should be able to expect a parent or an adult to look after them and keep them from harm wherever possible. That made it doubly hard to find a child dead or severely injured.

Of snoring and practical jokes

In the night room at Mather Avenue there used to be about 18 bunks. As new boys, when we arrived we had to pick a bunk that didn't belong to one of the firemen who had been on the station for a number of years.

I snored, though I was not the only one. One night I awoke suddenly from a deep sleep due to a pressure on my chest. One of the older firemen was trying to stop my snoring and threatening to finish me off if I didn't shut up. Needless to say I didn't sleep very well that night.

Snoring is always an issue with a group of people bedding down under one roof. Many firefighters snored to such an extent that those unable to get to sleep because of the noise slept in other areas of the station, away from the large night room.

It was the summer of 1967 and The Beatles were flying high in the music charts and had just recorded the song 'Penny Lane'. In the song there are references to the "fireman rushing in from the pouring rain"; he has "a clean machine"; and "in his pocket is a portrait of the Queen".

One day a television film crew from the BBC 'Tonight' programme turned up when Red Watch at Mather Avenue were on duty, and asked if they could film "the fireman rushing in from the pouring rain" – another line from the song.

The only problem was that it was a hot summer day, so the rain was produced from a hose reel as one volunteer ran across the yard to be soaked.

All the crew was filmed polishing the fire engine, and then one fireman pulled from his pocket a threepenny stamp that featured the Queen's head.

Japanese and American tourists used to turn up regularly asking if they could take photographs, but our boss wasn't having any of that.

At this time the operations of a fire brigade were like a closed book to the general public. Not many people knew what went on behind the fire station doors.

It was only years later with television series such as 'London's Burning' or 'Chicago Fire' that people realised the different emergencies that firefighters had to deal with on a daily basis.

Airport duties – not all fire related

I was dealt a miserable shock three months later, when a decision was made to move the Emergency Tender from Mather Avenue to Banks Road – and six firemen had to move with it. The old maxim of last-in-first-out was applied, and together with two other former junior firemen, I was posted to Banks Road along with three totally unwilling volunteers.

Banks Road was awful for us. The station was bigger but even quieter than Mather Avenue. The watch numbered around 30 firefighters because it covered the firefighting duties for the Garston area plus those for Liverpool Airport, whose main runways were less than half a mile from the rear gate of the station yard.

I was really distressed about it because it could be weeks before you were on a fire engine on the city side and even then the chances of turning out were very slim, as our fire engines still had to cover the airport.

Things were really bad if you were on the airport fire engines: you had no chance of going anywhere. In those days there were only a dozen or so flights a week to and from Ireland via Aer Lingus or to and from the Isle of Man in propeller aircraft.

However, I do remember one funny incident that occurred on a sunny afternoon. I was on the pump and we were told to report to The Barn, which was the airport fire station situated next to the new runway that Liverpool Airport had just built.

When we arrived, the Station Officer in charge of the airport fire station told us to follow his Land Rover as he drove from the gate opposite the station to the new runway.

About 450 metres *(1500 feet)* from the gate and on one of the taxi-ways parallel to the new runway there stood a young bullock. The animal had escaped from the farm that bordered the runway fence, and the farmer and his lad were trying with great difficulty to coax the animal back to the farm.

There were three of us firefighters and two airport security guards there to lend a hand. The Station Officer suggested that we tie two ropes around the bull's head, and then the airport guys and the Station Officer would man one rope on one side and two firemen and I would man the rope on the opposite side.

The farmer's lad was pulling the bullock from the front from the ring through its nose.

The farmer was at the back, slapping the bull's backside with a big stick.

The bull dug his feet in and firmly refused to move, so we tugged away, and it slowly began to move sideways towards my side of the rope.

At this point I noticed that we were edging closer to the metal perimeter fence that bordered the taxiway.

The other two firemen were also weighing up what would happen if the bull continued to drift in our direction and applied any speed. There was a good chance we could be forced through the railings like chips.

The airport security guys were also wondering: "What if the animal suddenly took off and those three firemen let go of the rope?" They realised that if so, they could be pulled for miles.

Then suddenly the bull stopped. It was snorting away and was not happy with being slapped on the behind. Having stopped and seeming to survey the situation, without warning it took off like an Olympic sprinter, flattening the farmer's lad.

We three firemen let go of the rope in an instant and so did the two airport security guys.

The only one to keep hold was the Station Officer. In his crisp white shirt and officer's cap he was dragged across the grass like a scene from an old cowboy movie. He shouted to us to hold on, but by this time we were flat on the grass doubled up laughing.

When the bullock realised that only one person had tried to stop it, he came to a halt.

The Station Officer picked himself up and came towards us looking like a giant grass stain and asking why we had let go of the rope.

Quick as a flash one of the airport guys said we had all been taken unaware as it dashed off.

Eventually we all picked up the rope again.

This time the bruised farmer's lad decided it was safer to hold the rope than pull the bull from the front and eventually we managed to get the beast off the runway.

The airport rescue boat

The airport fire crews were used to training days where they launched the inflatable life raft into the River Mersey. One of the airport crew would steer the boat, but it had to be crewed by the pump crew from Banks Road.

I had never been in this boat before, so I was thrust forward as the first 'volunteer'.

After donning a wetsuit I climbed into the boat. Three other 'volunteers' followed and off we went into the Mersey. The guy steering the boat had served in the Royal Navy and was puffing on a pipe as we made our way through the water.

After about 20 minutes or so we headed back to the launch point. En route we were instructed by the fireman steering the boat, that one of us had to jump overboard as we neared the launch point, grab the short line of rope at the front of the boat, and pull us to shore.

One of the firemen jumped over the side and swiftly disappeared under the water. He came up once gasping and spitting out water and disappeared once again.

I was becoming a bit worried for my colleague at this stage but no one else seemed to be taking any notice.

As the unfortunate soul was on his way down for what surely would have been the last time, the guy steering the boat grabbed him with a boat hook and pulled him back on board.

When we finally reached the launch point it was discovered that the wetsuit worn by the fireman had a number of tears in the fabric, so as soon as he entered the river, the suit filled up with water.

I made a mental note for future reference: Do not go in that boat again, under any circumstance.

After about 18 months I couldn't stand the boredom of Banks Road and the airport, and put in for a posting. But before I got my move to another station, another animal event happened.

An unexpected canine hazard

I do not like dogs and for some unknown reason they don't like me. One night on the pump at Banks Road, we turned out to a fire in a yard at the back of a factory. Someone had seen smoke and flames and dialled 999.

The officer in charge told us to put a ladder up to the factory wall, climb over, and put out a fire burning in the yard.

Together with another fireman, I climbed over the wall and into the yard. We had been there for no more than 60 seconds when I heard the sound of dogs running towards us in the dark.

My instinct was get out of there immediately. With a couple of leaps I was on a pile of pallets on to the wall and down, without even using the ladder.

My colleague unfortunately wasn't so lucky and was bitten on his bottom (I thought) by one of the dogs. He was taken to hospital for stitches and a Tetanus injection.

For many years I kept the secret from him that I had heard the dogs and was so busy climbing out that I didn't alert him.

When I finally owned up, he said that if it made me feel any better, when he got to the hospital the dog had actually bitten his inner thigh.

The doctor in Accident and Emergency told him that another inch and it would have torn his femoral artery and he would have quickly bled to death.

CHAPTER TWO

Massive tyre blaze

After what seemed like an eternity I was granted my posting and sent to Belle Vale Fire Station, which had only opened some three years earlier.

The station was massive at that time, and would later become the Divisional Headquarters with many admin and fire safety staff based there. But when I arrived there were just two fire engines and lots of rooms - and loads of toilets.

In 1970, on one beautiful sunny Sunday afternoon, both fire engines turned out to a fire in Woolton Quarry, about a mile or so from the station.

As we drove towards the incident, within a very short time the visibility was down to about 50 yards. Thick black smoke covered all the roads leading to the quarry.

When we arrived, there was a fire in a single storey shed inside the quarry with flames threatening a stack of tyres.

For many years old tyres had been dumped there, and in some places the stacks of tyres were more than 20 feet high.

The boss decided to use a hydrant outside the quarry entrance, but that was broken. We needed large quantities of water.

The problem with rubber tyres is that when they burn they give off oxygen, increasing the intensity of the blaze.

Assistance messages were sent, and at the height of the fire, about an hour after we arrived, about 25 fire engines from Liverpool, from the Wirral on the other side of the Mersey and from even further afield were tackling a massive fire.

In the early stages of the blaze, I was on a stack of tyres with two colleagues directing a jet of waters onto an area of fire when almost without warning the flames danced along the stack towards us. We had to drop the hose, jump down, and run towards safety as fast as we could.

It took 24 hours to bring the flames under control, and for many months after the fire crews had to stand by at the quarry while the remains of burnt tyres were cleared off the site.

The Liverpool Echo newspaper headline the next night was 'The Blaze That Shut Out the Sun'.

For weeks afterwards when you reported for duty, whether night or morning, there was the smell of burnt rubber in the locker room and engine house.

Keep Clear

Belle Vale Fire Station had been opened because the Ford Motor Factory in Speke had become a major employer on Merseyside, and many council flats and houses had been built to accommodate the work force.

Every morning, from about 6.30a.m., there would be long queues of cars blocking the exit from the fire station as the workers headed for the car factory. Naturally there was concern that we might be delayed in attending a house fire unless something was done.

At Belle Vale I was posted onto White Watch and my boss was a man called George Darcy. Stories about George were legend in Liverpool Fire Brigade. He was a real character and one whom I will never forget.

George had been captured by the Japanese at the fall of Singapore in the Second World War. He was sent to the infamous Prisoner of War Camp at Changi.

Eventually the Japanese instituted a simple rule: If you worked you got food, if not there was none. As many people were so debilitated by disease and starvation, food sharing by those to whom it was allotted to those who needed it became a way of life.

Prisoners from Changi were shipped to various places to work, including on the Burma Railway. George must have had a terrible time, and it is amazing how he survived.

There are many unprintable stories about his antics in the fire service, and I think his attitude of irreverence to authority and natural inclination to be a joker might have helped his survival during wartime imprisonment.

Now, faced with this increasing risk of vehicles blocking the entrance, George put pen to paper and asked senior management for yellow hatched boxes to be put in front of the station to allow us to have access so we could respond to emergencies as quickly as possible. The yellow hatch is a universal highways marking in Britain to show that you must always leave that space free of vehicles to allow cross access.

A few weeks later a man in a suit turned up outside the station together with two other men in a van. The three men stood in the road outside the station gesticulating in various directions, and pointing first this way and then that, up and down the road.

The man in the suit then left the scene and George went out to investigate. He approached the two men standing in the road and asked what was going on. In the finest of Irish accents they told George they had been tasked to mark 'Keep Clear' on the road in two places to solve our issue with vehicles blocking our route.

This was a challenge for George. His response gave authenticity to his nickname of 'The Weather Man'– so named because he often 'caused waves and clouded the issue'.

He said to the two workers that, given what they were about to do, when you drove along the road the first word you would see is 'Clear'. So he thought it would be prudent to put 'Clear Keep': then, as you drove up the first word you would see would be 'Keep'. Having caused confusion, George returned to his office and shut the door.

I watched the two workmen in deep discussion. About 20 minutes later the doorbell rang and I answered the door. There was the man in a suit, very red faced.

"Is the Station Officer in?" he asked.

"Follow me," I said, and knocked on George's office door.

The man charged in and said: "Mind your own business. My workmen are daft enough, without you sticking your oar in." He then turned on his heel and left the station.

If you drive along Childwall Valley Road to this day in front of the fire station on the road there are clear instructions to 'Keep Clear'.

To be a fire engine driver

Shortly after this, I decided it was time to add another string to my bow and become a fire engine driver, so I volunteered and spent three weeks on an HGV driving course (Heavy Goods Vehicle). When that was completed I then spent four weeks delivering fire kits and other items to fire stations and other facilities throughout the city, and only then was I allowed to drive back from fires.

Only when the Station Officer was happy could I finally drive to fires and other incidents.

Learning from the experience of others

All my life as a fireman, and later as an officer, I was always a good listener. I taught myself to learn from both good officers and drivers and also from bad officers and drivers.

I remembered a story from a very experienced and good driver who had been in the army, stationed in Germany a few years after the Second World War finished.

He told me about a incident when he was driving an army truck with half a dozen soldiers aboard. He was driving down a very steep incline when the brakes failed. When he shouted that the brakes had gone - every one of his colleagues jumped from the truck, leaving him on his own to try and bring the vehicle safely to a halt.

"Never tell them the brakes have gone," was his advice to me.

One balmy evening, when driving the pump responding to a fire-call off Bowring Park, I was about to slow down and turn left when the brake pedal went down to the floor and the machine shot past the turning.

"You should have turned left there," said the officer in charge.

"I know another route," I said.

By now we were travelling up hill and the vehicle was slowing down. I moved the automatic gearshift to low gear and managed to pull the vehicle up by hauling on the handbrake.

"What's going on?" the crew enquired.

"The brakes have gone," I confessed.

To a man they all jumped out onto the pavement. About 90 metres *(300 feet)* earlier we had been doing 50 m.p.h.

Is all clear?

One dark night, while out in the station area, we received a fire-call to 'chicken sheds' at the rear of Cobden Street in Woolton Village about a mile from Belle Vale Fire Station.

I was driving the pump as we drove into neighbouring Quarry Street we could see a fire burning behind the row of terraced houses.

I pulled the fire engine up by an entrance to an alleyway leading behind the houses and the crew pulled the hose off and disappeared down the dark alley to tackle the fire.

About two minutes later George Darcy arrived with the pump escape, as they had turned out from the station while we had been closer to the address. George went off down the alley to investigate what was going on.

Alerted by the blue flashing lights and the noise of the fire engine and the pump as it supplied water to the hose, a crowd had gathered in the road.

I heard a woman asking if anyone had seen her son but thought nothing of it, thinking her son was a youngster and that he was in the crowd. A few minutes later, the woman was back again, a little more frantic this time. In response, people were turning around looking for a youngster in the crowd. By this time, the fire had been extinguished.

It was very dark at the rear of the houses and the guys were dragging the hose back toward the fire engine. One of the older firefighters on the watch came to give me a hand closing down the pump and disconnecting the hoses.

I told him about the woman and asked if he had seen any young children behind the houses watching the blaze. He said the only people there had been the fire crews but he would check. He took a torch down the alleyway. A minute or so later he returned and shouted to the boss, George Darcy: "You had better come and look at this".

George and the rest of the crew followed down the alley. Shining the torch on to the pile of smouldering timber, the fireman pointed to the badly burnt body of a man, aged in his late thirties. This turned out to be the woman's missing son.

In another five minutes we would have left the scene. Imagine what would have happened the following day when the body was discovered.

I put it down as another lesson learnt: Never, ever, leave the fire ground until you are certain that the fire is fully extinguished and you have not missed anything at all.

This was quickly reinforced by another strange incident. Turning out well after midnight to an address off Childwall Valley Road not more than a quarter of a mile from the station, we found that, when we reached the end of the road, the house number we had been given didn't exist.

George Darcy checked with Control and they said the first caller had been confused with the road names but a second caller had said 'Chislehurst Avenue', which was even closer to the station.

Turning around quickly, we arrived at Chislehurst Avenue to find two tenants on the ground, incapacitated after jumping from the first floor windows into the garden. By then, a severe fire blazed in the ground floor rear lounge.

I was wearing breathing apparatus and went into the house to fight the fire using a jet of water. Everything was severely burnt in the lounge except one armchair that had been immediately behind the door into the lounge. The chair was moved outside during the firefighting operation.

The casualties in the garden had broken bones from jumping but were not seriously injured and were removed by ambulance to hospital.

After an hour or so, having put the fire out, we secured the premises and left the scene, returning to the station to clean our kit and the appliances and replenish the breathing apparatus sets.

An hour or so later, we turned out again to the same house. Smoke was pouring out from behind the boards we had used to secure the premises.

The officer in charge of the pump which arrived before the Pump Escape that had the boss on board realised that questions would be asked as to how another fire had occurred so quickly. To cover for the boss, he sent a message to Control stating that it was a rubbish fire outside the property, not knowing that a member of the public had rung the fire brigade asking why the first fire had not been extinguished properly.

It turned out that the armchair that I had removed in the first instance had been put back into the house before it was boarded up, but must have been still smouldering.

Anyway, the Divisional Officer on duty had been rudely awakened at home by Control and informed that a second call had been received to the property, so he made his way to the site to find out what was going on. As he turned into the road it was clear that the fire was not outside the house as had been reported and he made a beeline for George Darcy.

"What's going on?" he demanded, seeing the chair being brought out of the house - not knowing it was for the second time.

I had to explain that I had removed the chair the first time but didn't know how it was put back in the building. That was when George made a big mistake.

"I put it back inside the property", he said.

"What on earth for?" asked the Divisional Officer.

"Because it was raining, and I didn't want it to get wet" said George.

"Well it's bloody well wet now," said the Divisional Commander, storming back to his car.

George managed to escape any discipline charge, but the officer in charge of the pump who had attempted to cover for the boss got a rollicking for sending an incorrect message.

CHAPTER THREE

The power of silence for critical focus

We did have some grim jobs at Belle Vale during the four years I was there.

One night when I was off duty, the watch turned out to a removal van that had overturned due to thick mud on the road on a part of a housing estate under construction.

The removal van had furniture and a piano on board. As the vehicle skidded, it started to tilt and fall onto its side.

The driver stayed in his seat and wasn't badly hurt, but the guy in the passenger seat decided to jump out and was crushed and killed by the van.

Some months later, we turned out in torrential rain to a traffic accident on a road in the same estate. A minivan had skidded and gone under a lorry going in the opposite direction.

The passenger had gone through the windscreen and was dead in the road. The driver was trapped in the vehicle, which was crushed under the back axle of the lorry. A midwife on her way to a delivery had gone under the lorry and was trying to give first aid to the driver. The minivan gearstick had gone through the man's neck and it took us about an hour to cut him free. Unfortunately, he died on the way to hospital.

It was a very difficult, dirty and wet job to rescue the driver and I remember that, during the protracted attempt, very few words were spoken as the crew, together with the ambulance service, did everything possible to save the driver's life.

The ring of pain

One incident where I did more damage than good also happened during my time at Belle Vale.

One afternoon a young woman came to the station with a young child, her niece. The child had been playing with a piece of metal from the leg of a coffee table when it became jammed on her finger. The aunt had tried to pull it off, and tried soapy water without success, so she asked for our help.

We had a ring cutter on the station. It was used quite often to remove wedding rings when they could not be removed by any other means. Using this we tried to cut the metal but it was very tough.

The little girl was screaming by this time, so the Sub Officer suggested I went in an ambulance with the woman and child to the Children's Hospital. At the hospital an injection could numb the finger while I cut the ring off.

When we arrived at A&E I was in my fire tunic and it was very hot. A female doctor asked what I was doing there, and I explained that I had the tool required to cut the metal ring. She gestured to me to get on with removing the ring.

I asked if it wasn't a good idea to give the child a pain-killing injection first, but the doctor said 'No', so I began to cut the metal. What no one knew was that the metal ring had a serrated edge inside used to grip the wooden leg of the coffee table. As I was cutting the ring, the metal was cutting into this poor child's finger even more. I was sweating profusely and everyone was waiting for me to finish the job.

Usually when you cut through a wedding ring you would slide a piece of string on either side of the cut and pull the ring so that it opened out releasing the finger.

Because the metal was very strong, when I cut through it I was pulling with all my strength to open it up and release the little girl's finger. Suddenly the metal broke and my left hand smacked a nurse on the nose. She went down to the floor in a heap.

As the pressure released from the trapped finger, the blood from the wound hit the ceiling. The child was hysterical, and I was covered in sweat and blood and deeply embarrassed for knocking the nurse out.

Manning the boat

In the early 1970s I had decided to sit the promotion exams. I had wasted a number of years since my posting to Mather Avenue and several of my peers had been promoted, so I felt it was now time to get on the promotion ladder.

Having passed the Leading Fireman's exam when I was at Mather Avenue, I now tackled the Sub Officer's written and practical examinations. In 1974 I passed both at the first attempt, and now sought my first promotion and a chance to be in charge of a fire appliance. I received a phone call congratulating me on my promotion and I was informed that I was posted to… there was a pause… the Airport.

Noooooooooooh, not there. I wanted muck and bullets.

So a few weeks later I turned up for my first duty at The Barn – called that because it previously was one, but had been rather insubstantially modified with plasterboard walls and an engine house that was open at all times to the elements.

The station had three vehicles: the Land Rover that was driven by the Station Officer; the Pathfinder, a huge appliance that carried a thousand gallons of foam; and the (inflatable) boat.

As the new rank on the watch, the first thing I noticed was that I was the youngest by at least 15 years. The Sub Officer had served with the Civil Aviation Authority until Liverpool Fire Brigade took over responsibility for the Airport. The Station Officer was a lovely man and a dead ringer for Captain Mainwaring out of 'Dad's Army'.

On one unfortunate occasion he called me a silly boy over something, so adapting the TV series and later the film, I became known as the character 'Leading Fireman Pike' and the Sub Officer was the character 'Sergeant Wilson'.

The Station Officer was convinced that one night there would be a plane crash when he was on duty. He gave me strict instructions on one of my first days on duty that when I was making out the roster for the appliances for day or night duty there were three rules to follow:

- Fireman Dave had to drive the boat.
- If he was off, Fireman Jimmy had to drive.
- If they were both off, Fireman Kenny could drive.

About two months after I arrived I was making the board out for the following night when I noticed that all the named drivers for the boat were off: one was on a course, one was on holiday, and one was on sick leave.

I knocked on the boss's office door and went in.

"Sorry Boss" I said, "but Dave, Jimmy and Kenny are off, so who drives the boat tomorrow night"?

"Oh no," said the boss, "this is terrible." He put his head in his hands.

I made my way into the mess room and said to the firemen sitting there, "The boss is in a right stew. All the nominated boat drivers are off tomorrow night".

One of the assembled crew said, "I can do it Leading Fireman".

Thinking I had solved the dilemma I motioned to him to come with me. After knocking on the office door, I made my way in, followed by the enthusiastic volunteer.

"Problem solved boss", I said. "Fireman Bobby has had nautical experience; he can drive the boat tomorrow".

The boss took his head from his hands and looked up. "Have you had nautical experience, Bobby?" he asked.

"Yes boss. I have read *The Cruel Sea*".

I had forgotten that the walls were only plasterboard and the whole crew had heard my conversation. Bobby and I were quickly ejected from the office.

The boat was supposed to be launched into the River Mersey if a plane crashed into the sea. It had a crew of four men when launched and had all kinds of equipment inside.

To be honest, if a plane had come down in the Mersey, it would have taken many trips back and forth to rescue survivors with this one small boat.

Barn haunting

The Barn became famous in the local press because of very strange goings on. I don't know how it began but remember that nearly all the firefighters had been in the services and in a number of wars. They were practical fellows not prone to fantasise about anything.

One night, one of the firemen said he woke up to find a ghostly figure at the foot of his bunk. He sat bolt upright, and the figure disappeared.

A few nights later the ghostly figured appeared to a different fireman on a different watch.

Then it all blew up when a young fireman who was on detachment from another station for one night duty was heard to shout out a few times during the night.

When the watch members were showering and shaving the next morning, one of them asked if anyone else heard the lad shouting out. Someone suggested that perhaps he was having a nightmare.

Just then, the young lad walked into the washroom looking terrified and asked if they had heard him cry out. He said he woke up to find a ghostly figure of an old man pressing on his chest and shouted to the figure – who, he thought, was one of the watch messing about – to leave him alone. Realising finally that it wasn't a prank, he said he had sat bolt upright all night, too terrified to go back to sleep. His parting words were that he would never come back to The Barn again

Following this episode, some bright spark had an idea to bring in a Ouija board. During the session the ghostly figure allegedly said his name was 'Tom the Turnpike' and he had been hanged for a murder he had not committed. He said that his grave was in the farmer's field at the rear of the Dunlop factory, near to the station.

Acting on this information, three firemen went to the alleged spot in the snow one winter and said The Lord's Prayer over the man's grave. This action seemed to calm down sightings. But one hot summer day a few years later, when I had returned as the station officer, we had to do a boat launch.

The station now had a cleaner called Harry, who lived nearby and had a dicky heart. We left the station and returned about an hour later to find Harry sitting on a bench outside the station looking very pale. Thinking he was having a heart attack, I asked what was wrong, and if he was in pain.

Harry explained that he was cleaning the corridor in the station with a brush when a cold wind came down the corridor and physically pushed him out through the front door.

The door was always held open with a large piece of concrete. The concrete chunk was now lying just over 9 metres *(30 feet)* from the closed front door.

Harry was obviously frightened. He wasn't the sort of person to play jokes or make things up, so how had he ended up outside and how had such a large piece of concrete flown 9 metres on its own from where we had left it?

It was a total mystery, but the local press loved the stories and we received letters from strange people all over the country coming up with theories about what had taken place.

At the Barn, because there was very little to do, on a night shift the guys used to stay in bed until shortly before their reliefs came on duty. It was quiet and in the winter it was very dark.

The station had a milkman who used to deliver milk for all the watches every other day. When I first arrived at the station the milkman used to leave the crate of milk outside the station so as not to disturb the sleeping crew.

A few months after my arrival we had a new milkman, a young guy who was very loud, not just when delivering the milk crate. Instead of just making the delivery, he used to come in the station and shout comments such as "Get up you lazy bastards, here's your milk. I have been up since four o clock and you are all fast asleep".

A couple of the firemen decided the milkman had to be silenced. One time when he arrived at the station it was a very dark winter's morning and, to his surprise when he walked into the station singing at the top of his voice, all the watch were up and standing in the station office.

The milkman continued talking in his loud voice and verbally abusing one of the guys he knew on the shift. He also loved to tell tales about how he was giving more than gold top milk to some of the ladies on his round. As he went on about his fantastic stories one of the guys slipped out of the office and put on his large black duffle coat and a death mask.

The fireman climbed into the cab of the milk float and waited for the loud milkman to return to his vehicle. While he was waiting, he had put a number of ice cubes into a glove on his left hand.

The milkman left the station and we all rushed over to the window to see what was about to happen. He didn't notice the fireman in the dark duffle coat until a freezing cold hand was placed on his hands on the steering wheel. When he saw the death mask, he took off and ran back into the station. White as a sheet and gasping for breath, he fell to the floor in the corridor.

It was only when he saw us all standing there laughing loudly that he realised it was a prank.

After calling us all a shower of bastards, he flew out of the door, jumped on the milk float and drove off. He never came into the station again after that and left the milk in a crate outside.

Tough and realistic national training

It was 1976, and I was at the Fire Service College in Moreton in Marsh, Gloucestershire. As a junior rank in the fire service you had to attend a number of courses before you would be considered for promotion.

The first course I attended was the Juniors Officers' Course that lasted six weeks. Each week you travelled to the college on Sunday night and travelled back on Friday afternoon.

The College had every type of fire engine, the very latest equipment, and a huge airfield. Every day, different fire ground incidents could be set up to test your ability, judgment, and leadership qualities. It was unique and required hard physical effort to tackle some of the fires that the college staff set up for you to quell.

As well as this being tremendous experience that you couldn't otherwise gain, the other benefit of attending the College was that you met officers from all over the country and benefited from talking to them and listening to how they had dealt with various types of incidents in their own brigade.

The social side of the course was good, and we all went out as a large group and visited as many of the country pubs we could slot in during the six weeks. The Cotswolds is a lovely place to visit and the locals were very friendly because, of course we were spending a lot of cash in their community.

When I had finished the course I was posted from The Barn to Belle Vale on Red Watch. A few hours after I arrived we faced a massive fire involving tyres at company called United Reclaim in Speke, near the airport.

Now, 1976 was a very hot summer. The firemen attending that fire suffered badly from dehydration due to temperatures in the high 80s. They were wearing heavy fire fighting kit in the extreme heat from the burning tyres.

At the height of the blaze, when there were 100 firemen tackling the blaze, one senior officer thought it would be a good idea to give the guys salt water to drink to replace body fluids. This resulted in a lot of firemen vomiting up within minutes of drinking the solution.

Great example of a superb boss

I enjoyed Red Watch at Belle Vale: there were some good lads there and the boss, Bert Whittlestone, was superb. He would help you by passing on his knowledge, not only when dealing with fires and other emergencies such as traffic accidents, but in the way he dealt with the issues that the guys under his control brought to his desk.

We attended a fire one night in a block of apartments and Bert told me to get a ladder and pitch to some windows in case we had to make a quick exit or rescue anyone inside the block.

I detailed my crew and they began to take the ladder off the pump. I was telling the driver to send a message to control and assumed that my crew was getting on with the task.

When I looked around, one firefighter was having difficulty unlocking the ladder of the roof. I jumped up and helped him and finally the ladder reached the position where the boss wanted it.

When we were back on the station the boss called me into his office and asked if there was an issue with the ladder, and I explained what I had done.

I left the office, but was called back about half an hour later.

Bert told me that he had interviewed the fireman who was having difficulty unlocking the ladder and had found out that before coming on duty he had spent the afternoon in the pub. Bert left him in no doubt what would happen in future if he had reason to believe he was incapable of carrying out his duty because he had been drinking.

In dealing with the matter, no one else was involved, just Bert, me and the fireman concerned. It stayed that way.

I learnt a great deal from that station officer who later rose through the ranks to become a Senior Divisional Officer.

Promotion

Promotion came again in 1976 with a move to Banks Road, again this time on White Watch. I arrived with another new Sub Officer. Neither of us wanted to be at Banks Road for a long time and we both set about sitting and passing the Station Officers' examination.

It was good to work together, reviewing old examination papers, reading the syllabus, and when we were on duty, taking the opportunity to test each other.

When the examination day came around we had studied so hard that nearly all the questions were exactly what we had hoped for, and we both passed.

Now opportunities were open to both of us, as there were only four guys in the brigade with the Station Officers' ticket. As soon as a Station Officer attended the Fire Service College someone had to take his place on that station. It was a case of: Pack your kitbag and off you go.

My first posting was to Mather Avenue in charge of White Watch, finally returning to where I had started in 1966. I only had six weeks to spend there, but managed to witness another fatality in somewhat bizarre circumstances.

We were on day duty and turned out both machines to Greenbank Park, one of two lovely parks about a mile from the fire station. When we arrived, the park was totally empty of people. This was unusual but there were no obvious signs of a problem.

Then two young men in civilian clothes approached the machine and asked if I was in charge. They showed me their police identity cards and asked me to follow them, alone. We set off towards the park lake. When we arrived, one of the police officers pointed into the water and asked if I could see a body. Staring under the water I could just about make out a face and arm floating under the weeds.

The policeman asked if we could recover the body with as little disturbance as possible in case there was a murder weapon such as a knife that we couldn't see from our position.

The body was in about four feet of water, too deep for our usual fire protection drip pants. I remembered the old submersible suits at the airport and asked the police if they could send a car to pick up two suits and then we would be able to assist.

While we were waiting for the suits we split the nine metre ladder *(almost 30 feet)* into two sections and lay it in the water on either side of the body to act as handrails for the firemen in the water. The suits were duly delivered; and when the guys were kitted up, we got a plastic salvage sheet under the body like an envelope and dragged it to the side of the lake, where all hands pulled it out of the water.

It was a particularly sad case – not a murder, just a young man aged 18 taking his own life by drowning.

Two months later, I was off again, this time to Conleach Road Fire Station in Speke. When I arrived at a new station I always had a chat with the watch, and told them the standards I expected while I was in charge for the next six weeks.

When I finished the chat I always asked if there were any questions or if anyone had anything to say. This time there was a comment: "We heard about the fatality when you were at Mather Avenue. You are a bit of a jinx. Can we have a fairly quiet six weeks, please?"

About two hours later were attended a serious fire in a joinery workshop where I had to send for assistance and it took 20 firemen an hour to bring the blaze under control. Not a good start.

On the next tour of duty we had a fire in a block of two-story apartments in Speke at lunchtime. It was 365 metres *(1200)* from the station, so when we arrived the firemen were still putting on their breathing apparatus. The front door was open and there was quite a bit of smoke in the hallway.

I spotted a young woman standing at the top of the stairs and shouted to her to follow me. But she was frightened, so I ran up the stairs, grabbed her and pulled her with me back down and out into fresh air. I asked if anyone else was in the building and she said no.

The fire was caused by a chip pan and quickly extinguished. We were just tidying up when a police officer asked me if the baby was okay. I asked which baby, and he replied "The baby the young woman threw out of the first floor window to neighbours down below".

My experience was beginning to tell me that you should always expect the unexpected, and then you will never be surprised.

A week or so later we attended a huge blaze in a block of apartments in the same suburb. Sadly, it set a precedent for the months to come.

The block of apartments was run down and quite a few were empty and had been vandalised. The residents who still lived there were desperate to be re-housed, but no one was listening to their pleas.

About quarter to six one evening I arrived with the two machines to find a large area of roof space ablaze.

The roof was circular and covered a large area. It transpired that there was no separation at all in the roof space.

The fire quickly spread, and the tiles were exploding with the heat and raining down on the firemen below.

I sent an assistance message for the turntable ladder to tackle the burning roof area.

Because of the water we directed onto the roof space, a number of habitable apartments were damaged and now the residents had to be found new accommodation.

A few weeks later there were three similar fires in other blocks in Speke.

Word had spread to residents that, if they wanted to be re-housed, everything would be sorted if they set fire to the roof space.

I was on the move again in early 1977, this time to Old Swan Fire Station in charge of White Watch.

My very first night on duty was the first major blaze at The St John's Shopping Centre in the city centre.

We weren't called to the fire in the early stages but we covered most of the city instead, fighting fires in three other areas because those crews were at St John's Precinct.

From turning out at 18:00 hrs we finally returned to Old Swan after midnight to be told that we were on the 02:00 hours to 06:00 hours standby at St. John's, and I was in charge.

The standby crews were there to make sure that all pockets of fire had been extinguished and there was no chance of re-ignition.

When we arrived there was all kinds of looting going on, with vans being loaded with washing machines and anything else that people could carry.

There was an early police presence but that was increased significantly to deter any further looting.

After the fire, Merseyside Fire Brigade recommended to the precinct owners that sprinklers be fitted during the re-building.

That advice was ignored and in 1979 the building was severely damaged once again by fire.

Sprinklers were eventually fitted.

CHAPTER FOUR

The Firefighter Strike

There was a major problem looming for the fire brigades across the country, as the demands for a decent wage for firefighters were rejected by the Labour Government.

Due to this, something I believed would never happen did. On November 7th 1977 the fire brigades went on national strike.

I thought it would be over within days. A strike had taken place in Scotland in 1974 and the Conservative Government had given all firemen a £7 a week rise to return to work.

This time the army was called in to cover for the firefighters. When the strike began we had a lot of public sympathy and financial support as we picketed outside the various fire stations.

I picketed at Derby Lane Fire Station where public support was first class. On a Friday afternoon a few of us used to go to the local industrial estate with large empty plastic sweet jars. As the factory workers finished their shifts they used to fill the sweet jars with money for the striking firefighters.

A few weeks into the strike a couple of children died in a house fire. As a relative of the family used to work in the Old Swan industrial estate, we were told not to turn up any more for money.

Public support began to drain away. I was desperate to return to work but there was no end in sight, money was running low and, like most firemen, I didn't know which way to turn.

There were a number of officers who didn't strike and the venom and hatred aimed at them when they turned up on the fire ground was unforgiving.

It was the worst time in my career and I honestly thought that it would never happen again in my lifetime after this first time.

In January 1978, after nine weeks of strikes, we finally returned to work for what we had been offered shortly before the strike began. There was bitterness and a sense of being beaten.

In the weeks following the return to work there were arguments, fights and damage caused to equipment on stations, but the worst thing was a sense of despair.

Traditional union men resigned their posts and allowed left wing socialists to take their places. No one turned up for station union meetings. It was the start of continued disruption for many years to come

There were promotion boards held some months after the return to work, but of course the jobs were offered to the officers who had remained at work during the strike.

Temporary Station Officer Posting

In January 1979, the fire brigades across the country changed their shift patterns resulting in an additional watch on each station. So on January 1st 1979, as a temporary Station Officer, I took charge of Green Watch at Banks Road Fire Station.

We worked two 9-hour day shifts then two 15-hour night shifts, and then were off duty for four days.

The lads on Green Watch were a good bunch. I had two excellent Sub Officers who ran everything. All I had to do was manage the day-to-day issues that might arise. It was the start of a fairly uneventful 18 months.

Airport Fire Officer's Training

In early 1980 I was put onto an Airport Fire Officers Course at Stansted Airport. There were officers on the course from Heathrow, Gatwick, from airports across Europe, and from Israel. It was an intensive course and most enjoyable.

One of the more hair-raising exercises we faced was sitting in one of the mock-up aircraft on site while they filled it with cosmetic smoke. When the aircraft was full of smoke we had to find our way to the exits. It was extremely challenging to do so. It made you realise the extreme difficulty in evacuating a fully laden plane filling up with smoke and possibly flames following an accident. Perhaps that was a contribution to my intense fear of flying.

Following my attendance on this course I was asked to volunteer to go back to The Barn as the temporary Station Officer, with a promise of a substantial post in the near future.

I took the plunge, and in October 1981 I was finally promoted to the rank of Station Officer.

I had visions of being at the Barn for many years because I held the Airport Fire Officers Certificate and there were only two other officers with that qualification. But a surprise was just around the corner and the start of the most amazing years of my firefighting career.

At first it was just a rumour that the Liverpool Airport Authority wanted to employ its own fire crews, and then it came to reality. We were told that on April 1st 1982 all the firefighters and ranks at The Barn would be posted to other stations in the Merseyside Fire Brigade area.

Where would I be going this time?

When the station closed, at first there wasn't a vacancy for me to fill, so I spent a couple of weeks at Old Swan.

My own watch at last

Then one afternoon I received a phone call from a 'mole' at Central HQ telling me that I was going to Blue Watch at Toxteth, and adding tersely: "Good luck with that."

I was ecstatic. Finally I had my own Watch on a very busy fire station, which had only one fire engine and a turntable ladder. I was looking forward to it, although I knew that eight months previously there had been major rioting in Toxteth when tear gas was used for the first time on the streets of England.

I also knew that there lots of old properties dating back to the 1850s that had been converted into apartments. There were many rows of terraced houses and many ethnic minorities crammed into sub-standard blocks of apartments. These were all the things that had increased tensions before exploding into violence and destruction of shops and buildings in August 1981.

On the tour before I was to start at Toxteth May 13th 1982, the Senior Divisional Officer rang me. He said there had been problems with Blue Watch at Toxteth but I was not to go in there with a big stick. If I needed help, I was to let him know. What was all that about? I hadn't heard of any issues. There had been nothing on the jungle telegraph. So began my first tour at Toxteth.

The station was a large Victorian house in Belvedere Road, with wooden sheds in the rear yard that housed the fire engine and the turntable ladder. The kitchen, mess room, my office, the snooker room and the watch room were all on the ground floor. The locker rooms were on the first floor, and the night room was on the second floor.

On my first parade, we were one man short. No phone call was received, and so began my first problem. I asked one of the night watch to stay behind until I could sort out where the missing fireman was.

Ten minutes later the absentee walked passed my office door pushing his bicycle. I wished him good afternoon and got a smirk in return.

"Would you come into the office"? I asked. He sauntered in.

"Why are you late for duty"?

He replied: "Only 15 minutes."

"In those 15 minutes we could have turned out to a house fire, someone could have needed rescuing and we were a man down."

"It won't happen again," he replied.

"If it does, you will be on a charge. Now get your kit on the machine and check all the gear." Was this the big stick I wasn't supposed to wave?

At lunchtime I walked into the mess for my dinner. As I sat down, one fireman put four cans of lager on the dining table. "What are you doing?" I asked.

"Having a drink with my dinner," was his response.

"No you are not," I said

"You can't stop me," he replied.

He was technically right. At that time there was nothing in Brigade Orders about drinking alcohol when on duty. However, there was no way I was going to allow any firefighter under my command to drink alcohol on duty and I had to make a stand.

I picked the four cans of lager off the table, and told the fireman to put them in his locker and take them home at six o' clock. I then told the whole watch, and especially the drivers, that if I suspected that anyone was unfit to carry out their duties or we were involved in a traffic accident, I would ask the police to breathalyse them.

I was beginning to see what I was up against.

Blue Watch at Toxteth on May 13th 1982 comprised 1 Station Officer, 1 Sub Officer, 1 Leading Fireman, 5 drivers and 5 Firemen.

Within 10 years one driver and one fireman would die of alcohol problems.

The station received around 5,000 calls a year. With just one fire engine, every time we turned out we had to have back-up from one of three other stations.

The important thing to remember was that normally we were on our own at least for five minutes at every fire, traffic accident, or other emergency. All the crew had to be 100% fit and able at all times. If we were one man down, it could cost us all.

Two weeks after I arrived I recorded that we had attended about 8 to 10 calls each tour so far, ranging from building fires to car fires – and there were lots of car fires.

Fire in Ritson Street

One Saturday night in those early weeks, we turned out to a house fire in Ritson Street off Lodge Lane, the scene of the 1981 rioting and only about half a mile from the fire station. There were reports that the occupier was trapped inside.

As we approached the street of terraced houses, each connected to the wall of the one either side, we could see flames above the rooves.

Ritson Street is very narrow, one of three similar streets in Lodge Lane. Those streets were built in another century, with allowance for passage of a horse and carriage, and not for modern day car parking, so now there were cars parked outside the houses. The driver turned left into the street.

We could clearly see flames sweeping across the road, above the house involved and threatening the houses on either side. We had to drive slowly to avoid removing every wing mirror of every car parked half on and half off the pavements.

I could see people banging on the doors and windows and kicking at the door, trying to get into the house next door to the one on fire.

I told two firemen to put on breathing apparatus and get a jet of water to knock the fire down and try and get in the house on fire to try and rescue the occupier. The other fireman was told to come with me, get into the house next door and remove the occupants.

The driver had to set into a fire hydrant in the street because we were going to need more water than we carried in the tank. I had called for assistance as we drove down the street.

The vehicle stopped. The two firemen hit the burning house with the jet of water. I ran with the other fireman and we kicked the door in to find an old man lying on the floor just behind it. We dragged him out and I told the fireman to give him oxygen.

At that precise moment the bay window of the burning house fell out, hitting both firemen and knocking them to the floor.

A hand grabbed my shoulder and dragged me backwards towards one of the neighbours who was lying on the pavement. This man had tried to get into the old man's property by breaking the glass quarter-light in the door and had severed the artery in his arm. Blood was spurting into the air.

Now, at this point in the films, Superman usually appears and saves the day. But this was real and this was me. I put my fire boot on the man's arm and pressed down.

A police officer ran towards me and asked if I needed help. There was an ambulance speeding down the street towards us, so I showed the policeman how to put pressure on the severed artery and said that this guy was the priority when the ambulance stopped. Then I turned to see the two firefighters stagger to their feet. They gestured thumbs up – they were okay.

By now the old man was breathing okay and another ambulance was on the scene to look after him.

Finally, now assistance had arrived, we could gather our thoughts.

There was no one in the burning property.

The old man had been too frightened to open the door when people started banging, because he had done that some weeks earlier to knocking and been robbed.

In the following months, work commenced on demolishing rows of terraced houses in the area to replace them with better housing and so new smaller blocks of apartments could be built. This all followed the previous year's riot.

Unfortunately, the demolition companies used to set fire to the empty houses about five o clock every day in the winter months. They were not supposed to do this, and it meant that we would turn out to find a number of houses blazing.

It was dangerous enough firefighting, but the buildings were liable to collapse without warning. While firefighting one night we were on the first floor of a house when the floor collapsed.

Three of us managed grab hold of something to prevent us ending up in the basement. Months later, at a similar incident, an officer was not so lucky and ended up in hospital for a few weeks.

You had to fight the fires from inside because children used to play in them and vagrants would sleep in them, so you could never be sure that they were empty.

The station had its first fatality soon after I arrived. About 8.30am one morning White Watch turned out to a house fire, in which a young girl died.

In November 1982 we moved into a brand new fire station to cover the Toxteth area, in High Park Street. On the first night there, we turned out at six in the morning to an apartment on fire off Lark Lane, a very popular eating and drinking area on the edge of Sefton Park.

We had been firefighting all the previous night from 6pm, as it was two days before Bonfire Night and fireworks had caused many blazes.

Within five minutes of arriving, the crew had broken down the apartment door, entered wearing breathing apparatus, and rescued and resuscitated the occupant, who was unconscious and hanging out of the bathroom window, desperately seeking air.

I knew that the firefighters on Blue Watch could be difficult to manage. But on the fire-ground where it mattered, they worked together like a well-drilled team and they were spot on.

We received a letter of Chief Officers Commendation for that rescue. The new station had been christened with its first rescue, and there were many more to follow in the years ahead.

Upper Parliament Street chip fire and arson

Towards the end of 1983, I had my first fatality in Toxteth in an old Victorian building in Upper Parliament Street, a once grand street full of houses of a type that would have belonged to a rich merchant in the early 1900s.

In recent times these houses had been divided with bad construction into poorly appointed small apartments.

In this case the property had one staircase which served all four floors. This meant that a firefighter had to gain entry through the third floor via a hydraulic platform appliance.

The heat was tremendous because the firefighter was necessarily positioned above the fire as the heat made it difficult to go down the staircase to fight the fire from above.

On arrival there was a severe fire on the first floor which restricted access and egress via the staircase. Very few of the occupants spoke English and it was difficult to know if anyone was still in the building.

I sent an assistance message for three additional fire engines, withdrew the crews from the upper floors, and concentrated on working our way up the staircase from the ground floor to search floors one and two.

During that firefighting operation, three firemen were injured by falling debris or exhausted through the physical effort required to gain access up the staircase.

Crews managed to reach the second floor and determine that none of the apartments on that floor were still occupied.

The first floor fire was now under control and we began to pick our way through the debris along the first floor.

Finally we reached the last room on the floor. Lying on the remains of a bed was the body of a man. The room was next to the communal kitchen and the deceased, or one of the other residents had left a pan cooking on the stove and that had caused the fire.

The following week we rescued a woman from a first floor flat in a similar residence nearby. A passer-by had spotted the flames.

Looking through the letterbox of the flat I could see smoke and flames. Then I saw a woman standing there. I shouted to her to open the door but she shook her head and walked off into the flat.

We battered the door down with a sledgehammer and two firefighters in breathing apparatus carried the woman out to a waiting ambulance.

Upon investigation, it proved that there were three or four seats of fire in the flat.

The woman was later arrested and charged with arson.

CHAPTER FIVE

Explosions and smoke inhalation

In 1984 The International Garden Festival opened in Toxteth on the site of what had been a huge waste tip. This event was the brainchild of Michael Heseltine. The idea was to counteract some of the negative press about Liverpool following the Toxteth riots. When opened, the Garden Festival attracted many visitors from all over the world.

In that year, Merseyside Fire Brigade attended over 41,000 calls for assistance.

One fire I will remember for the rest of my life occurred on Sunday March 29th 1984 at 18.02 hours.

We responded from Toxteth to an assistance call from the two machines from Canning Place Fire Station. They had turned out to a large single-storey factory which was unoccupied.

The Sub Officer who was in charge told me that when he arrived there were a number of small fires outside the factory, but inside one of the loading bay doors that had been damaged and there was a lot of smoke.

I decided we would commit men inside the building in breathing apparatus and with jets of water to check if there was a fire inside. One crew consisted of my Leading Fireman and one firefighter. The second crew made up of a Sub Officer and another firefighter.

The crews entered the building, and within a short time the amount of smoke you could see through the loading bay door had disappeared.

Two senior officers had arrived by this time and they took charge of the incident. The Sub Officer who had been in the building came out to tell us there had been a number of small fires inside. These were mostly wooden pallets but they had been extinguished and there were no other fires visible.

It was decided to send another team of firefighters inside in breathing apparatus to open the remaining loading bay doors and clear any remaining smoke.

The third team had just entered the building when thick black smoke suddenly appeared through the loading bay doors. We needed to evacuate the building immediately.

To evacuate a building you use your whistle. I ran to one loading bay door and the Sub Officer from Canning Place went to another door, blowing our whistles.

Two crews came out very quickly but there was no sign of my crew. I crawled down under the smoke layer in the loading bay door to see if I could spot them on their way out. After another minute or so a figure stumbled through the smoke towards me. It was the firefighter. We pulled him out of the building. His fire tunic was smouldering. His ears and the side of his face were burnt around the mask he had been wearing.

I asked him where the Leading Fireman was. He said they had been a few feet apart in very little smoke when he heard a noise like an express train, followed by a blast of heat and he was blown over. He had picked himself up and followed the line of hose to exit the factory. He was taken to hospital in a waiting ambulance.

We carried on looking for the Leading Fireman. A few minutes later he appeared. His tunic was on fire, his gloves had been burnt off, and the skin from his hands was hanging down.

We soaked him with a hose reel. The breathing apparatus set he had been wearing was badly burnt and we took it off his back and rushed him to another ambulance at the scene. His life lay in the balance and his firefighting days were over.

I remember stumbling around the factory in a sort of daze. The factory roof was exploding and huge flames were shooting into the air. I couldn't believe what had happened, how had a fire that was under control suddenly turned into a raging inferno?

A senior officer approached me and said I should return to the station and he would let me know about the injured members of my crew as soon as he heard anything.

There was only myself and one firefighter left from the crew of five that had turned out over an hour before. The driver had gone in the first ambulance with the injured firemen.

I had to drive the machine back to Toxteth.

Nothing was said. We were both numb.

When we returned, the turntable ladder crew had heard about the fire and asked about their colleagues. I told them all we knew. I then went into the toilet in my office and burst into tears.

My face was blackened by smoke. My eyes were red and stinging, and as I breathed my chest was very sore. I pulled myself together, washed my face and changed my clothing, but my breathing was laboured.

There was knock on the office door. It was the remaining fireman from the crew. He didn't feel well and had a severe headache. Ten minutes later both of us were in an ambulance on our way to The Royal Liverpool Hospital.

We were split up on arrival. He went one way and I was wheeled into X-ray on a trolley. After the X-ray, I was asked if I had ever had tuberculosis – a question that frightened the life out of me. It turned out to be something to do with the X-ray plate being fuzzy.

A doctor examined me and suggested I should go home and have a good night's sleep and see how I felt in the morning. A senior officer arrived at the hospital and drove me home.

It was 9 weeks before I was able to return to work. My lungs were congested and for three weeks I couldn't even walk to the end of the street.

My own doctor wasn't any help but finally sent me to see a chest specialist at Broadgreen Hospital, who discovered the problem was with my lungs. Following lung function testing he prescribed asthma inhalers and tablets. Those 9 weeks were dreadful. I thought I might never return to work as a firefighter.

As for the Leading Fireman, his life hung in the balance for four or five weeks. At the Royal Liverpool Hospital it was obvious that the Leading Fireman's burns were severe, so he was rushed immediately to the specialist Burns Unit at Whiston Hospital a few miles away.

When someone receives severe burns, the normal treatment is to carry out skin grafts from other parts of their body, but when the Leading Fireman arrived at Whiston Hospital they discovered that in the extreme temperatures the sweat under his fire kit and clothing had turned to steam. His whole body had been scalded.

I went to visit him within a few days of the incident. The smell in the Burns Unit cannot be described. It entered your nostrils as soon as you walked through the ward doors. Within minutes it had reached the pit of my stomach and I wanted to retch.

The staff efforts were magnificent, but we knew it would be touch and go for a number of weeks.

One of the Burns Unit Sisters asked about the gloves we had worn on the night of the fire. I told her they were like gardening gloves you would buy from a supermarket: cardboard cuffs, cotton backs and slightly stronger palms.

The Sister explained that it had taken a long time to remove the cotton from the gloves out of the burnt skin. She said she was no expert, but surely we should have better hand protection for fighting fires.

Some months after the incident, the Fire Brigade Union on Merseyside conducted trials on six different types of gloves used by neighbouring fire authorities. The gloves were sent to the six busiest stations in the Brigade, together with questionnaires asking which gloves were best for heat resistance, penetration by glass or metal, sensitivity of touch, and what happened when the gloves were wet.

At a meeting of Merseyside Fire Brigades Health & Safety Committee that I attended, the results of the survey were announced. It was unanimous which glove passed all the criteria needed to provide better protection.

The Assistant Chief Fire Officer who chaired the meeting, gathered up all the paperwork, praised all concerned for the survey and as he reached the door on the way out, announced that we could have the cheapest pair.

Everyone was stunned. What to do?

The Fire Brigade Union rang every fire station and said any firefighter who sustained a hand injury, cut or burn while wearing the present gloves was to put in a claim. Within weeks, claims soared.

Eventually the best gloves were supplied.

There was never an inquiry into the fire. I was never asked to attend and detail what actions I had taken and why. It was many months later I read in a magazine that the factory had been a former cold storage depot. It had long been vacated, but had been broken into and fires started inside and out.

A small part of the interior wall had been damaged and the fire had burnt the insulation behind the wall, travelled up the wall into the roof space. Here, it had burned without being visible until it flashed over and burst through the roof at a temperature of 1,000 degrees into the main factory area where my crew were preparing to leave, thinking the job was complete.

The Leading Fireman had some fingers amputated and his hands were an ugly sight. He never returned to do the job he really loved, getting stuck in to fighting fires.

A blood bath

The year 1985 started with a bang, or rather a collapse. One winter's morning we were due to finish the shift when instead we were turned out to investigate a collapsed wall at a house in Salisbury Road.

When we pulled up outside the address there was no sign of an outside wall collapse, so I knocked on the front door. The door was opened by a frail old lady who was covered in dust. She motioned to follow her into the room at the rear of the house in which the air was thick with dust and soot.

There on the floor was the chimney-breast wall – every last brick of it. The debris covered the bed in which the lady had been sleeping and most of the furniture. There was a gap in the ceiling, through which I could see the bathroom above.

The woman was distraught as she feared her cat was under the rubble.

We had to shore up the ceiling before starting to remove the rubble off the floor. A building surveyor arrived and said the collapse had been caused by the extremely cold weather. Leaking water from damaged gutters had got into the joints between the bricks and expanded.

We carried on lifting up the rubble, expecting at any minute to see a flattened cat, but when we moved the lady's bed, the cat had been hiding underneath it and wasn't injured. The headline in the Liverpool Echo that night was: 'There goes my bed'.

In May of that year we turned out to a house on fire in the same road as the fire station. It was about 10.30pm when we arrived at the address.

There were flames visible in the front room window and the front door was open. As I walked up the path to the house with two firemen in breathing apparatus carrying a hose reel, there were footprints in blood going in the opposite direction.

I told the firemen to knock the fire down and search the house. I followed the trail of blood to the house next door and shouted inside, "Hello?"

A voice responded, "She's in here."

I walked into the house and could hear people talking in the back kitchen. Then a woman ran into the room shouting: "I'm sorry. I'm sorry." She was naked, her face was black with smoke and she was bleeding severely from huge cuts on her arms, her stomach and her legs.

Trying to appear calm, I said: "Don't worry. Everything will be okay".

I raced outside and told the driver to request an ambulance immediately and then get the First Aid Kit and try to cover and put pressure on the wounds.

Looking back to the house that was on fire, I could see the two firemen waving to me. I ran up to them and through their breathing apparatus masks they told me the back kitchen was covered in blood. It was on the floor, the ceiling, everywhere.

I promptly asked the police to attend. Five minutes later two detectives arrived and I took them into the kitchen to find it awash with blood.

The police thought someone had been murdered, as there was some human flesh on the floor as well.

An ambulance had arrived and the injured woman was rushed off to hospital.

The fire had been extinguished so we left the police to investigate what had happened and returned to the station.

About 1am the station doorbell rang and when I opened it there was a policeman standing there. He said the Inspector had asked him to fill in the details of what had happened in the house before the fire.

The injured woman had been released that morning from a mental hospital. Upon release she had been informed that due to the medication she was taking, under no circumstances was she to drink alcohol.

The woman's partner had picked her up from the hospital and taken her straight to the pub, where they had stayed until tea-time. Then on the way back to the house, they had bought a Chinese meal. They had eaten the meal, leaving the wrapping paper on top of the hi-fi player next to an electric fire. Then they had taken their clothes off and fallen asleep.

The paper had fallen on to the fire and ignited.

Some time later the woman had woken up coughing from the smoke from the fire.

She had tried to wake her partner, but couldn't. She then had made her way into the kitchen to escape the fire but the back door was locked.

The key was kept on a hook at the top of the door, but in the smoke she couldn't locate it.

In desperation now, and choking, she smashed the glass in the kitchen door with her arms and screamed. Two men in a garden nearby heard the scream.

They jumped over the fence to see the woman leaning through the broken glass and smoke pouring out behind her: they dragged her through the door.

Hearing the screams, her partner woke up two or three minutes later.

On reaching the back door he faced the same problem and they also dragged him through the broken glass.

That was where all the blood came from.

Thankfully, both made full recoveries from their injuries.

CHAPTER SIX

The gas fire explosion

In 1986 at 04:06 on August 29th there was an almighty explosion that was heard not only on our fire station, but miles away. Then the loudspeaker system sounded. We turned out to Grinshill Close, a road containing newly constructed houses.

As we approached the address, people were running in their nightclothes in neighbouring streets. The machine turned into the Close to see a scene of utter devastation. Where there had been a terrace of four two-storied houses that were only about 12 months old – house numbers 10, 12, 14 and 16 Grinshill Close - only one house appeared to be intact.

One house was badly damaged, and numbers 10 and 12 were just a pile of rubble, with people desperately tearing at the mound.

I had remembered a story from my time at the Fire Service College from an officer who said that he had arrived at a multiple car crash on the motorway. Seeing the extent of the devastation, he parked his vehicle on a bridge over the incident and made an assessment of what was needed for assistance. He said that if he had driven down to the crash scene, survivors and relatives of victims would have grabbed him and pulled him this way and that, preventing him from taking charge.

On this night I had the Sub Officer and Leading Fireman riding in the back of the machine. They jumped out with the rest of the crew. I locked the door and sat and looked at the scene in front of me. People were grabbing the torches from my crew and they were being pulled this way and that by desperate neighbours.

I reached for the radio and sent an assistance message for four more fire engines and the Emergency Tender. I also asked for the urgent attendance of the police for crowd control. Only then did I get out of the cab.

Trying to ascertain how many people we may be looking for under the rubble was near impossible. Some of the people digging had come from streets far away. Their windows had blown out, or their roof had been damaged by the explosion.

The first thing we did was set up lighting.

The police and the additional crews arrived within five minutes.

I blew my whistle to get the crowd's attention and pleaded with them to get off the pile of rubble. We needed to listen for anyone shouting for help under the wreckage.

I split the crews into teams. The police had the crowd helping by forming a chain as we passed sections of timber and rubble away from the pile.

We couldn't hear any noise from under the rubble, so it was decided to try and burrow under a section where there might be an air pocket. It was dangerous, because by forming a small tunnel it could collapse onto the firefighters crawling under.

One area yielded nothing at all, with a fireman going only a few feet before he reached a solid blockage, so we tried another route. A fireman from Canning Place burrowed his way along for some distance and shouted that he has found someone.

Everyone stopped and waited as he inched his way in reverse back to the entry point.

When he finally came out, he had found a large teddy bear.

Obviously in the dark, and with his gloves on, it felt like a body. Everyone started laughing, but the teddy bear was very large and looked new. I asked him exactly where he had found the toy and could he go back and carry out a thorough search in that location. Three or four minutes later he re-appeared with a nine-day-old baby boy, alive, but covered in dirt and dust.

The police had now ascertained that in one of the houses there may have been a woman with a new baby and her brother. I hoped that the mother would be close to where her baby was found. This time we widened the gap and lifted off surface rubble in that area.

Within a short time we discovered the baby's mother, trapped under an overturned bed which had formed an air pocket around her. She was brought out and taken with her baby to hospital. Remarkably, neither one was seriously injured.

Digging went on looking for the brother, who it later turned out, was not in the house that night. By now it was after 7am and light enough to see that there was no possibility of anyone else being under the remaining rubble, which was now only two or three feet high.

In all, 8 people had been injured in the explosion, 15 houses had been damaged, and 2 totally destroyed.

The Gas Board attended and quickly identified that a gas pipe had been cut through in one of the houses. The occupier of that house had asked a relative to disconnect her cooker to take to her new address. The relative cut through the gas pipe and told the woman not to turn the gas back on. She forgot.

The gas board estimated that for many hours gas had been filling up the house after the woman went out for the evening. In another house, the baby's mother had got up during the night to feed the baby. She switched on the lights and the spark had ignited the gas and caused the explosion.

Two men were later arrested and charged with causing damage estimated to be over £100,000. The story made the headlines in the local and national papers as well as national news on the television.

Crew bravery and commendations

While I was on leave in October of that year my Watch rescued 14 people from a block of apartments in another station's area.

Two of my crew were commended by the Chief Fire Officer for 'acting with great presence of mind and diligence despite the severe conditions, in safely evacuating the occupants of the apartments involved'.

Arson and fires set accidentally by children

The year of 1986 was only two days old when we responded to a fire call to a house in Belvedere Road at 21:00 hrs. It was a multi-occupancy building built in the 1890s, like many in the area.

By the time I arrived the fire had been extinguished. Someone had put a small pile of rubbish against the front door of a first floor flat and set it alight. A young man staying with his girlfriend on the second floor had smelt burning and put the fire out with a bucket of water. The only damage was to a doormat and the flat door.

We started to remove the burnt rubbish when the flat door was opened by the occupier, an 88-year-old lady. When I told her what had happened she became distressed, so I took her into the flat to calm her down and I called for the police.

The old lady told me she had lived in the house for 15 years without any bother, and then some weeks previously, the landlord had let the ground floor flat to a young man and his friends.

The man's friends had smashed her windows on Christmas Eve and kept shouting abuse through her letterbox. The reason she gave was that the young man used to knock and ask her for food or money and she would send him packing. An old man on the same landing used to give them what they wanted for some peace.

Two female police officers arrived and confirmed that they had been called to the premises on a number of occasions recently. They asked the old lady why she didn't move to another flat. She defiantly answered that she had lived in the area all her life and no one would force her to leave – the only way she was going to leave was in a wooden box.

I left the police officers to take a statement and departed about 22:00 hrs. About an hour later, I turned out to the same address. This time the ground floor flat occupied by the young troublemaker was well alight, with flames shooting out through the windows. The rest of the building was heavily smoke logged.

A group of young girls were on the pavement outside, screaming that people were trapped inside the ground floor flat and on the upper floors.

Realising that it might be some time before assistance arrived, I put on a breathing apparatus and set along with three of my crew. I told two of them to take a jet of water and tackle the fire and then search the flat on fire.

The other fireman and I went up to the first floor to evacuate the old lady and anyone else up there. On the first floor landing we found an old man collapsed at the head of the stairs. We carried him outside into the cab of the fire engine, where the driver gave him oxygen until an ambulance arrived.

The assisting crew had arrived and they were sent to rescue the old lady from the first floor.

It transpired that the young guy who had put out the first fire – and knocked on the old ladies' door when he realised how bad the second fire was – had taken her out of the building via the first-floor fire escape at the rear of the building. No one was in the ground-floor flat. The old man and lady were taken to hospital for a check-up and later released.

The police arrested a number of people throughout the night. One young man was charged with arson. The trial took place 18 months later. I was called to give evidence and given a grilling by the defence barrister.

The barrister kept leading me towards an assumption that, because I had said the majority of fires I attended in Toxteth were arson, I naturally assumed that this fire was deliberate, when in fact it had been caused by an electrical fault.

I responded by stating that if I went to two fires in the same building within a year, I was suspicious. If I went to two fires in the same building within two hours, I was convinced there was an arsonist.

No further questions were fired in my direction.

The trial lasted for several days until it was thrown out on a technicality over the way the defendant had been questioned by the police.

I know the old lady still lived in the building in 1989 when she was 91 but now she had moved to the ground floor.

One month after that incident we carried out another rescue that earned Blue Watch Toxteth and Blue Watch Canning Place a Chief Fire Officers Watch Commendation.

On a Sunday afternoon we responded to another multi-occupancy building fire, this time in Parkfield Road, a four-storied Victorian house on the edge of Princes Park. The first floor was ablaze when we arrived.

While the crew ran out some hose, I made my way to the first-floor landing. There was a severe fire in a first floor flat.

The flat door was open, so smoke and flames were heading up to the second and third floors.

It took four lengths of lightweight hose that we carried on the machine to reach the first floor from the fire engine.

I told the crew to tackle the fire and then make their way upstairs to search the upper floors.

Another two machines had arrived and now six firemen in breathing apparatus began searching the building.

What we didn't know was that the residents of the apartments had put their rubbish in bin bags on the stairs and staircase landings, so when the crew left the hose on the first floor landing having knocked the fire down they didn't have any water supply to tackle the burning bin bags on the upper floors.

All credit to them: they carried on up the stairs and in a second floor flat located the resident, a man, unconscious on the floor.

The man weighed a bit over 95 kilos *(210lbs or 15 stone)* and had to be brought down the staircase for three floors through the smoke and heat.

It took a superhuman effort and for two firemen it resulted in back injuries, but another life was saved.

The rescued man worked at Liverpool University and was a well-known chess player. He was in hospital for two weeks and called in to the station after his release to thank the guys for saving his life.

Later that year we were presented with the commendation, which read, 'The Chief Fire Officer commends Blue Watch S6 High Park Street for their courageous and determined rescue carried out on Sunday 2nd February 1986'.

Once again we achieved our goal: to ensure that anyone who was alive when we arrived at a fire would be rescued and survive.

Sadly, just four weeks later, death gained some revenge. At 09:28 on March 6th we responded to a house fire on a new estate half a mile from the station. There, we were confronted by a number of hysterical people who said there was a baby trapped in a bedroom.

I made my way up the staircase while the crew pulled off the hose.

I could see the bedroom across the landing was on fire. There was thick black smoke containing molten plastic drops that were dripping down the walls. Without breathing apparatus I was unable to move forward. I hoped the baby was in another bedroom and not the one on fire. As I lay on the landing, two firemen came up the stairs carrying the hose.

A second fire engine had arrived and two more men in breathing apparatus went into the bedroom. They seemed to be gone a long time but it was in fact only a few minutes before I heard a shout from inside the room, then the sound of a crew running out of the bedroom.

I slid down the stairs. The smoke was choking and the plastic droplets were stinging my eyes. Then out of the smoke appeared a fireman carrying a blackened bundle, an 18-month-old baby girl. The fireman ran to a waiting ambulance, but I knew it was too late. Within minutes the police informed me that the baby was dead on arrival at the hospital.

The bedroom that the baby had been in was severely damaged by the fire, but on investigation we could establish that it seemed that the cot had been set on fire. Around the house there were loose matches in most of the rooms. It was believed that the baby's three-year-old brother had been playing with matches and had set fire to the cot.

My son, John, was six months old on the day of the fire. How could I stop him from playing with matches or lighters in the future?

The death of that baby left its mark on me and I will always remember that fire until my dying day. I had never had a child fatality in a fire before.

I had rescued children, had children overcome by smoke, or suffering burns, but never a death.

The birth of Phil the Fire Engine

There was nothing that I knew of in the education system to help children understand the dangers of fire and playing with matches.

I decided to write stories for children that would explain to them what a firefighter's role was in their community, how firefighters tackled fires and traffic accidents; and provide fire safety advice that they could easily understand.

I used to sit in my office late at night, deciding on the best way to get the important message across. There had to be a central character with whom boys and girls could readily identify and remember the name.

I thought of a fire engine taking that role, because I thought that almost no matter where children live in the world there is a fire engine that will respond to a fire in their road, their house, their school.

What could I name the fire engine so children could remember and say the name? What name rhymed with 'fire engine'?

In the station office one night I was looking at the firefighter names on the watch roster board and I noticed that three men had the same first name: Philip.

That would do it. I would call the fire engine 'Phil' because to children the 'P' and the 'F' of 'Phil the Fire

Engine' make the same sound. So 'Phil the Fire Engine' was born about six months after that baby's death.

A few weeks later after a very busy night, we responded to a flat on fire about 06:00 hrs. By the time we arrived everyone had managed to escape. The occupants were a mother and three children.

The mother said to me that her three-year-old son was always playing with matches and had started the latest fire. She asked if I could have a word with him.

Hiding in the alleyway I found a little black boy with lovely curly hair. He was obviously frightened. I gestured to him to come to me but he turned and started to run away.

I whipped my fire tunic off and caught him after 18 metres *(20 or so yards)* and picked him up in my arms. In his panic he peed over what at the start of my shift had been a clean white shirt. It was now black from various smoky fires attended during the night.

I told the boy I wasn't going to hurt him, and told him how dangerous it was to play with matches. I asked if he knew that in a fire, his mum and brothers could die from breathing in smoke.

After a few minutes he said he wouldn't do it again. I then went back to the mother, explained what I had said and asked her to make sure not to leave matches or her lighters lying around where the little boy may be tempted to play with them. Talk about igniting an explosion. The mother went berserk, telling me, with a number of expletives added, to mind my own business and not tell her what to do with her matches and lighters. It seemed there was just no helping some people.

I don't know what happened to the little boy, whether he became a full-blown arsonist or took my advice, but he would get little help from his mother.

CHAPTER SEVEN

A case of mistaken identity

A most unusual fire I attended happened later in August that year. Turning out to a shop on fire in Mather Avenue station area, we found it blazing.

Flames were sweeping out across the busy road and as it was the evening rush hour the traffic had to be stopped.

Straight ahead I could see a man's body lying in the side street next to the main road where the shop was.

I told the driver to pull up in the side street. The man obviously had serious head injuries and I told one of the crew to see what he could do with some First Aid and to call an ambulance urgently.

I carried on down an alleyway at the rear of the shop with the crew and started to tackle the fire with a hose jet. The premises that were ablaze sold children's clothing. There was a very strong smell of petrol in the shop and at the rear of the building. The blaze had spread rapidly but took about an hour to extinguish.

The injured man was taken to hospital and our investigation began to find out what had happened. It transpired that the injured man, the shop owner, had been closing up for the night when a man entered the shop and began calling the owner by another name.

The owner said the stranger must have the wrong shop and asked him to leave. The man then produced an axe and began to beat the owner about the head causing him to fall injured on the floor. While he was lying semi-conscious the axe man began to pour petrol all around the shop. The injured shop owner had crawled and dragged himself out of the rear door just as his assailant threw a match onto the petrol.

There was an explosion and the shop windows blew out. The building was quickly engulfed in flames. The shop owner continued to crawl along the rear alleyway and collapsed in the side street where we had found him. He eventually recovered from his physical injuries but he may never recover from the mental scars of his attack.

The shop owner had no idea who the axe man was looking for, and to my knowledge he has never been caught.

Rubber tyres ablaze

In October 1986 a massive blaze broke out at the Kirby Tyres site in the Speke district of Liverpool. From Toxteth we were turned out to assist the initial attendance of two fire engines at 12.30 pm.

The Kirby Tyres site comprised four very large single-storey sheds stacked to the roof with tyres of all shapes and sizes. Larger tyres, such as those used on huge diggers, were stored outside the sheds and in various places around the site. Lorries loaded with similar tyres were parked between the sheds.

There was very little space between any of the four sheds, and when the first crews arrived, number two shed was well alight.

I was told to take three crews and set up three ground monitors to try and prevent fire spreading to sheds one and three. The whole area around the site was known to have poor water supplies, so water relays had to be set up from larger hydrants well over half a mile away.

Water relays take time to set up with both fire engines and large amounts of hose required. If lengths of hose burst anywhere in the relay, it can take some time to replace them and during that time you lose your water supply and the fire spreads.

As with the Woolton Quarry fire described in an earlier chapter, rubber burns very fiercely and with great heat.

By the time the water relay was working properly, sheds one and three were involved. Over 100 firefighters were now trying to bring the blaze under control but despite us rolling huge tyres away from the heat, the flames eventually caught up with them.

By the time the fire was eventually brought under control, only number four shed remained. The blaze had caused £5 million worth of damage.

Once again, it was many weeks until the whole site was cleared by bulldozers, so crews had to stand by day and night until the operation as complete.

Local house fire with two survivors

One month later, we missed the first call to an address in our station area, as we were already engaged elsewhere. When we returned, we were re-directed to assist.

I was briefed by the Sub Officer who had arrived first. He told me that there had been a fire which they had extinguished in a ground-floor flat, but the building was heavily smoke logged.

We needed to put crews in breathing apparatus into the property to search for casualties. I took charge and asked him to organise the crews to enter and search.

I was standing in the garden when I heard a cry for help. I looked up and saw a man at a window in what I thought was the building next door. He said he was trapped by smoke entering in his flat and that the staircase was smoke logged.

Together with two drivers who were standing by their machines, we put a ladder to the window and rescued the man. It was then we realised that this was not the two separate properties it had been originally but one very large building with an adjoining corridor. In all we had to search 20 apartments.

Five teams wearing breathing apparatus were told that if they could not enter a flat, they were to break down the door and search thoroughly. One crew searching on the first floor could not enter a flat so, using a large axe, they forced entry. In a back bedroom they discovered a man lying unconscious on the floor.

One fireman removed his breathing apparatus mask to give it to the casualty, and he and his colleague carried the man down the stairs to a waiting ambulance crew, where he was revived by oxygen.

All the apartments were searched and no further casualties were found. The blaze was suspicious and the police were called to investigate.

We would return to these premises again.

Not just fighting fires

It was not just fires in 1986.

One evening we turned out to a newsagent's shop not far from the station. The shop owner had said there was a strong smell of petrol in the basement. Down I went, and there definitely was a smell. It wasn't petrol, but there was something.

The shop was in a terrace of similar premises, so I told each one of the crew to take a shop each and see if there was a smell in their basement.

I took the premises to the right of the newsagents, which was an undertaker. I knocked on the door and rang the bell a few times. Eventually, a man in a suit opened the door and I explained that I wanted to go into the basement.

Having gained admittance, I asked the man, who was very unsteady on his feet, if they had spilt any Formaldehyde in the premises. He said he didn't think so, but I could check.

As we entered another part of the premises the man's speech became slurred. He had obviously been drinking heavily. I asked him if anyone else was in the building and before I could stop him, he threw back the curtains in the room to reveal half a dozen corpses laid out in coffins waiting for funerals.

"Only me and these people in here," he said.

I thanked him very quickly and exited the front door, where I could tell by the smiles on the crew's faces they were glad they had gone down the block and not up it as I had.

Finally, we found the cause of the smell: an old oil-fired boiler in the basement of a derelict shop at the top of the block. Having ascertained that, there was no more responsibility for the fire service: it became a police matter.

Early in January 1987 another fire occurred at the very large house with all the apartments mentioned in the previous chapter. Red Watch from High Park Street attended and quickly dealt with a small fire started deliberately at the rear of the building. Once again the police were called to investigate.

On March 3rd at 02:07 hours a more serious fire call was received to the same address, to which Blue Watch attended. This time the whole of the back of the property was well alight when we arrived. All the occupants were running from the property, except two. These two men were having an almighty punch up. They were finally separated by the other occupants.

I recognised one of the fighters as the owner of the very first flats set on fire. He was also the same man who had called us out to a small fire at the rear of the building before the fire where we rescued two occupants. It was his flat that was on fire. Other residents told me that they had seen the man swinging the flat door vigorously in an attempt to fan the flames.

When I entered the building, there was obviously a very serious fire developing on the first floor. I knew the building would take a serious effort to search in such arduous conditions, so requested another four pumps to attend.

In all, fourteen men in breathing apparatus searched the building and extinguished the fire. Fortunately, this time no one was trapped, as they would not have survived.

The police arrived and I gave them all the information I had, pointing out the man whose flat had been on fire. As the police approached him, he tried to run away but he was detained, questioned, and later charged with arson. At the Crown Court he was found guilty and sent to a mental hospital.

During my time at High Park Street, we built up a good relationship with the police at Admiral Police Station which was 91 metres *(almost 300 feet)* away. We often needed their assistance when we were attacked en route to or during our fire fighting. The police there would call us out to deal with the numerous car fires they had to attend.

As a fire station, the enormously wide range of types of car on fire that we attended went from a Mini to a Rolls-Royce and from a Lada to a Porsche.

We also responded to the police station a number of times to cut off handcuffs when the keys had been mislaid.

In May 1987 we were called out to a fire in one of the police station cells. One of the prisoners had set fire to the mattress in the cell. Fortunately, the desk sergeant smelled burning and unlocked the cell door to find the prisoner unconscious on the floor.

By the time we arrived, the sergeant had dragged the man into a corridor.

We managed to revive the prisoner with oxygen before he was taken to hospital.

In my report I praised the actions of the sergeant for his prompt action, but he was disciplined for failing to discover the prisoner had hidden matches.

There are always good and bad people in all sorts of jobs, and the police force was no different.

One sunny afternoon there was a traffic accident at the junction of High Park Street and Windsor Street and we were called to swill away spilled petrol.

A car had driven through a 'Give Way' sign and hit a brand new van. The van had been shunted into a lamp post outside the Police Station, leaving the lamp post leaning dangerously over the busy road.

No one had been injured in the crash, so while my crew swept up broken glass and swilled away the petrol, I requested a lighting engineer to attend, so we could bring the lamp post safely down.

Although the accident was right outside the Police Station it was considered to be a traffic incident, so we had to wait for the Traffic Police to arrive.

A police car arrived and I asked if they had any traffic tape so I could cordon the road off until the lighting engineer arrived. They didn't have any, but said a traffic van was on its way and tape would be on there.

The van arrived and I asked the policeman for some tape, explaining why I wanted it. The officer looked me up and down in distaste and in an unpleasant tone said that he would deal with me later.

The policeman spoke with both drivers involved in the accident and then, together with the van driver, pushed the van into a position directly opposite the leaning lamp post.

The city lighting engineer had arrived. We had met before, as knocking lamp posts down was a game frequently played by the drivers of stolen cars in Toxteth. Normally, he would cut through the steel rods while we attached a rope, and, as each rod was cut through, the lamp post would slowly be lowered to the ground.

It usually took the cutting of three of the five supporting rods before the lamp post moved very much, but, as fate would have it, not on this day. As the first rod was cut, the lamppost began to swing wildly. We had tied a rope to it, but the lamp post was too heavy and it began to fall directly onto the van containing the unfriendly policeman. We shouted to him to move the van.

He looked up to see the lamp post heading his way. Frantically, he began searching his pockets for the keys. It was like a scene from an old silent movie as the lamp post continued towards the van.

The policeman found the keys, started the van and shot forward just before the lamp post crashed down exactly where he had been parked. Not only that, but it also crushed the van involved in the accident – the van that had previously sustained only minor damage.

As the police officer jumped from his van and ran towards me, I got the distinct impression he was upset. He demanded my name as he was going to report me for the damage to the van.

I responded: "Who was the daft sod who had put the van under the lamp post in the first place?"

It is often difficult at incidents to be civil and pleasant with everyone, particularly when you may be having a bad day, but it is always best to be pleasant with those who can be of great assistance and get you out of the mire.

We frequently turned out to assist the crews from Canning Place or West Derby Road fire stations as they backed us up on many occasions. One afternoon, we were in our station area checking on the fire hydrants when we were directed to a house fire off Myrtle Street near the city centre, which was actually Canning Place's area. As we were mobile, we arrived before the two appliances from Canning Place.

Driving down Myrtle Street, we found a man waving. He directed us into a service road behind a terrace of large houses off the main road.

As we pulled up we could see a fire at the rear of one property. One of the neighbours said they had seen a young man enter the house before the fire started, so my crew donned breathing apparatus and entered through the back door. Within a minute or so they carried out an unconscious youth of about 18 or so years of age.

The casualty had a weak pulse so we began resuscitation with oxygen and my driver requested an ambulance to attend. Shortly afterwards the youth stopped breathing, so together with one of my crew I began CPR while the driver chased up the whereabouts of the ambulance.

Control responded by saying that Ambulance Control said the vehicle was in attendance. The driver said it wasn't, that we were doing CPR and needed paramedic assistance immediately.

What we didn't know was that the crews from Canning Place had arrived at the front of the building and were tackling the blaze from there, not realising that we were at the rear trying to save the rescued youth. When the ambulance turned up at the front, it was much to the surprise of the officer in charge, who didn't know who had requested their attendance.

We were still administering CPR but the casualty's pulse kept coming and going and I thought we were going to lose him. From the crowd that had gathered and was watching our efforts, a man stepped forward and said that the casualty had taken a quantity of drugs. The drugs were having an opposite effect to the CPR we were administering.

Shortly afterwards, the ambulance found our location and the crew gave the casualty an injection to assist his heart. A few days later we were told that he had made a full recovery.

CHAPTER EIGHT

Introducing the fire station to the locals

I always considered my fire station to be part of the community. On a number of occasions we held fundraising events at the station for local hospitals or good causes. One of the favourite ones we held over the years was a huge jumble sale. All the Watches were involved and we got many kinds of goods donated by various stores, local businesses, and individuals. We stored these all over the station and in a garage in the station yard.

The day before the sale, we were overflowing and hoping that people would turn up.

No need to worry: about an hour before we opened the gates there was a long queue around the block and when we opened the gates we were nearly run over. It was a great success.

The fire station had always had an air of mystery about it. Not many people knew what went behind the electronic doors. Local schools would visit occasionally, but we never really went out into the community, which I thought was a fault that needed to be put right.

In the Toxteth area, the total number of languages spoken by the different ethnic groups was staggering. But, as a member of that community, any information we had to impart was in one language, English. This caused us a number of problems like the time we were called to a fire in garage adjoining a shop. The Indian woman owner of the shop had been burning rubbish in the garage. The side door of the shop was open and smoke from the fire went into the house, up the stairs, and filled the whole building.

A neighbour, thinking the garage was on fire, called us out. When I arrived, the Indian woman would not let me enter the garage, thinking she would be in trouble. Eventually I gained access and realised that the house was smoke-logged.

I asked the woman if anyone was upstairs but she didn't understand. Just then one of her older children arrived and said her younger sister was sleeping in the bedroom.

The child was quickly rescued by a team in breathing apparatus and an ambulance was called. But the mother wouldn't let the youngster be taken to hospital for a check-up as she feared the child would not return.

We needed to get the message out to all the people we serve in our community that we were there to help them.

Unusual fire engine freight

One very unusual request we received for assistance was three weeks before Christmas. It was from a local bakery in Lark Lane. The baker had made a giant chocolate Christmas Log with the intention of selling slices and donating the proceeds to the world-famous Alder Hey Children's Hospital.

The problem we had to solve, was how to get the large log from the first floor to the ground floor so that it could be cut into slices for sale.

The local papers and radio would be there, as well as a local actor who would encourage people to dig deep and raise funds for a slice of Christmas Log.

The night before the operation was to take place I was visualising us dropping the log leading to headlines such as *'Clumsy firemen drop children's cake'* or *'Sticky end to Station Officer's career'*.

We arrived at the shop in the fire engine and I had also brought the Turntable Ladder along to assist. The log cake was on a large board and was between 3 and 4 metres in length *(about 12 feet)*. The first-floor shop window was taken out and the Turntable Ladder extended to the first floor.

Six firemen and a couple of bakery staff slid the log onto the ladder and, when it was firmly in place, the ladder was slowly swung around until it was flat on the vehicle roof. Now we had to lift it down to floor level. It was very heavy but nothing fell off it as we successfully lowered it to the ground.

The TV personality cut some slices and the crowd that had gathered to watch the operation began to tuck into the log. Two hours later we had to transport a couple of buckets filled with donated money to Alder Hey together with the remains of the Christmas log for the children to enjoy.

The Turntable Ladder with the log lashed firmly in place took off in front of my machine as we made our way to the hospital. This exercise in creative logistics was successful. Apart from a couple of robins and some plastic holly, the Christmas Log arrived safely.

Helping the ladies

On a beautiful sunny afternoon I was turned out to assist someone locked out of their flat in Ullet Road on the edge of the station area. On arrival I was met by three "ladies". Two of the women were holding the other one up. I asked what the problem was, and was informed that the one being held up had had an epileptic fit, lost the keys to her flat and her friends had called the fire brigade to assist.

To gain access to a property, the procedure was to call the police. When the police arrived, the fire brigade would gain access and that would be the end of the matter.

On this particular day, when I requested the police, I was informed that due to operational commitments they were unable to attend. The procedure now was to knock on doors either side and confirm with neighbours that this woman was in fact the occupant of the flat to which we needed to force entry. But all the other apartments in the block were empty or boarded up. So we pitched a ladder to the second floor window.

One fireman went up the ladder and I asked the woman to describe what was in the kitchen to me whilst the fireman confirmed by looking through the window. Everything seemed to be in order so we broke a small window on the second floor and a fireman climbed in, forced the door lock from inside, and access was gained. The woman and her two friends went into the flat, thanked us for our efforts, and we returned to the station.

About 20 minutes later a police car arrived at the fire station. The policeman apologised for being unable to attend earlier but he had called at the flat in Ullet Road and spoken to the ladies and was assured that everything was okay. Ten minutes later I had a telephone call from Fire Control telling me that a woman had called the fire brigade and said that her flat in Ullet Road had been burgled and the fire brigade had let the burglars in.

The next event in the saga was a senior officer arrived at the station telling me what a silly boy I had been letting three ladies burgle the flat. I told him that I had followed procedure and on the evidence gained, I decided that the woman did in fact live at the flat, so I forced entry.

I asked what if I had decided that, as the police could not attend and there was no way of proving the woman lived there, I had decided not to assist. Then, after I left the scene the epileptic woman had another fit, fell and died. The headlines in the paper would have been 'Fire officer leaves helpless sick woman to die'.

Then of course there was the fact that the police had called at the premises and seen all the women there after I left.

The story then unfolded and the truth came out. The woman who was supposed to have had an epileptic fit was in fact an alcoholic. She did live at the property with her sister, who rented the flat and used to have the woman's benefit payments sent to there to prevent her from spending it on alcohol.

On the afternoon in question the woman had been drinking in a local pub and met her two accomplices. She explained that if she could get into her sister's flat, they could get the benefit payment and that would pay for drinks all night.

The two accomplices came up with the idea of calling the fire brigade to gain access. When they got into the flat those two decided that if they took other items from the flat they could have drinking money for a few days. So they pocketed a number of items.

On finding out all the information, the Fire Brigade decided that if the woman who owned the flat prosecuted her sister for burglary, they would pay for the damage caused by us gaining entry.

The woman refused, so the Fire Brigade said that the officer in charge had acted upon the information he was given by her sister and, to prevent any more distress to the supposedly epileptic woman, had forced entry, so they would not reimburse her for the damage.

Slow path to promotion

I had been at Toxteth now for getting on seven years. Officers had come and gone on the other three watches.

Some were high-flyers destined for senior officer positions. Junior ranks were sent to learn about the brigade the hard way. They didn't last very long.

All the other watches had had at least two or three station officers in the time that I had been there. So I was thinking about possibly being promoted to the next rank for the amount of fire and incidents I had attended. But it wasn't that simple. I later came to the conclusion that working in a very challenging area, putting out fires and saving lives counts for nothing in the case of promotions.

Unfair mantle of authority on a young officer

I had a young officer sent to join my watch for at least six months. He had been promoted to temporary Sub Officer at another busy station in the brigade. On the day he arrived at his posting the Watch Station Officer went off sick. So now the young man was in charge of a very busy station with a crew of men all many years older than him.

That day he had one of those never-to-be-forgotten days, with lots of calls, serious fires, and a fatality. He didn't get any help off the crew or sympathy because he was the officer in charge. It was his job to manage, even though he had very little experience.

The next tour of duty he went sick – call it stress, or fear, or doubting his own ability. Word went around the brigade that he couldn't do the job when the pressure was on. He returned to his normal quiet station for a few months and then they posted him to my station at Toxteth.

Before the shift started, the young man knocked on my office door, asked for a chat, and said that I had probably heard about the fact he couldn't handle the last posting he had.

I told him that it wasn't his fault. It was a mistake by senior management. The moment the Station Officer went sick at his last posting, a senior officer should have sent in an older experienced officer to help him through the tour.

Later that day, the Divisional Commander arrived on the station. During his visit I told him what I thought about the young man's last posting and my opinion on what should have taken place.

I was rebuked and told: "A monkey with two bars on its shoulder can do your job and be in charge of a fire engine."

That statement summed up an underlying problem with senior management. Yes, they may have been to fires before they became tied to a desk, but times were changing fast.

In their day the windscreens of the appliances were not smashed regularly; stones were not thrown by very young children; and people did not steal equipment off the fire engine while you were fighting a fire trying to save lives.

It had become a war, and we were losing the battle daily. Following the 1981 riots there were minor skirmishes and the occasional blow up when things got out of hand.

CHAPTER NINE

Firefighting in civil unrest

One night when I was on leave, there was an incident in Granby Street when a gang of youths began setting fire to a number of shops and stoning the police. My crew turned out but was prevented from attending the incident immediately by the Police Commander who said it was too dangerous and they could not guarantee the crews safety.

My very experienced Sub Officer said that there were shops on fire that were people's livelihoods. There were people living in the apartments above the shops whose lives might be in danger, and he wanted to talk to the ringleaders. He was allowed through the police cordon and drove down to the crowd in the street.

A lot of young men stopped the fire engine and asked what he was doing. He explained that he wanted to make sure no one's life was in danger and didn't want any trouble.

Some older men came along, talked some sense, and were just about to sort out the issue when the police came steaming down the street with loads of vehicles. Bricks were thrown and the fire engine windscreen smashed before the crowd was dispersed.

Later some of the older men came to apologise to my Sub Officer. They said they would have let him put the fires out but once the police arrived there was nothing they could do to control the younger guys.

The police said they thought the crew was in trouble so they came with all guns blazing.

When we used to attend stolen cars set on fire in the early years, the favourite dumping grounds were cul-de-sacs. We would turn into the area facing the burning vehicle, pull out the hose, and extinguish the blaze.

Then we would request the police to attend so that they could obtain the engine number and inform the car's owner that their vehicle had been discovered burnt out.

Eventually the locals cottoned on to the procedure, so they would wait behind a wall for the police to arrive and then unleash a barrage of bricks at our appliance and the police van .

So, after a dozen or so incidents we decided to reverse into the cul-de-sac, put the blaze out and inform the police at Admiral Street Police Station when we returned to our station. That way we reduced the risk of another windscreen being smashed.

How to grow £250 to £700

One night when I reported for duty the day shift, Green Watch, were out on a call.

About 17.45 Control rang the station and informed me that Green Watch had turned out earlier to a house fire, and as they were on route to the incident, some boys had launched a builder's plank at the fire engine from on top of a container.

The plank had smashed the windscreen.

Fortunately, neither the driver nor the officer in charge was injured, and they had continued on to the fire. I was asked to contact the local windscreen company who were by now on speed dial from the station.

About 30 minutes later, the replacement windscreen arrived and shortly afterwards the fire engines returned from the call.

Within a short time the screen was replaced and I was asked to sign the repairman's documentation.

Three weeks later a bill for £250 for the windscreen replacement arrived at the station, addressed to me. I put the bill in Dispatches to the Finance Department for payment.

Four or five weeks later a second bill arrived. This time it was for £400 for the same repair and there was a notation that as the first bill had not be paid within 30 days, the discount had been removed.

I rang the Finance Department and asked why they had not paid the first bill. No one remembered having seen the first bill and asked me to send the second bill to them immediately, which I did.

Two months later a County Court Summons arrived at the station addressed to me, stating that I had to appear in Bedfordshire County Court over non-payment of the invoice, which was now in excess of £700.

I rang the Divisional Commander and told him what had just arrived in the post and he laughed. Talk about 'light the blue touch paper'.

I told him in no uncertain terms what would happen if a County Court Judgment was issued against me. It would be headlines in the local paper that instead of Merseyside Fire Brigade paying a bill of £250 for the original invoice, they had cost the taxpayers another £500, and one of their officers had been served with a CCJ.

I heard no more about the matter.

It was probably no wonder that I was being overlooked at Promotion Boards after incidents like the windscreen saga, but I kept applying.

Rank doesn't always deserve respect

After another unsuccessful promotional application, I was sitting in my office when the Divisional Commander opened the door.

As normal I stood up and invited him to sit down. He said he wasn't stopping. He was on his way into town for lunch but had called in to debrief me following my last Promotion Board.

I invited him to sit down again. He told me that it wouldn't take long. He went on to say that I would never get promoted while I was breathing as I had only ever been operational and his grandmother could do my job.

I asked what his grandmother was doing on Saturday night, so I could take the night off. He raised his voice and told me not to get funny with him.

I told him not to get funny with me and asked how dare he, my Line Manager, debrief me in such a manner? He was supposed to point me in the right direction so I could obtain promotion, not belittle my rank and ability.

I told him to get off my station.

A few weeks later I had another large property fire and asked for five pumps to attend to assist in searching the premises. When an incident has five or more machines, senior officers are informed and normally they will attend.

Procedure was that when a senior officer attended an incident, the officer in charge would fully brief them. If the senior officer was to take over the incident he would inform the original officer and send a message to control that he was assuming command.

This particular night the Divisional Commander turned up in a suit and bow tie. He had obviously been attending a formal function. He made no attempt to speak to me but sent one of the drivers to tell me that he wanted me to report to him.

I told the driver that I was in charge of an ongoing incident, and if the Commander put on his fire kit he could join me on the fire ground for an update. The driver returned saying that the Commander was very angry and he was ordering me to report to him.

Once again I refused. If I left the fire ground there would be no Incident Commander.

Now the Divisional Commander stormed over to me, still in his suit. He said he was ordering me to send the 'Stop' message. Sending the 'Stop' message means that everything is under control, everyone has been accounted for, and the incident will be closing down shortly.

I asked if he was taking charge and he replied "No".

I responded that I was refusing to send the 'Stop' message until I was certain that the whole building had been searched and no one was trapped. Once again he said he was giving me an order and, if I refused, I would be on a charge.

At that point there was a commotion at one of the first-floor windows of the building on fire. One of my crew approached me and said that they had found a man unconscious upstairs and they were carrying him out to resuscitate him.

I turned to the Divisional Commander and told him that was why I did not send the 'Stop' message. He turned on his heels and went back to his function. I sent the 'Stop' message a few minutes later.

A new Chief Fire Officer was appointed a few months later and he quickly established which of his senior commanders should consider taking their pensions and retiring. The Divisional Commander retired.

Finally a proper promotion –temporarily

In 1991 a new Divisional Commander had arrived and I was asked if I would like a temporary promotion to Assistant Divisional Officer at Southern Divisional Headquarters at Belle Vale.

"Yes please," I answered.

So for nine weeks including Christmas 1991 I had my chance to show what I could do.

It was fairly quiet the first couple of weeks leading up to Christmas and I spent my time mainly dealing with paperwork from the stations in the Division.

I was on call on Christmas Eve, Christmas day and Boxing Day 1991. My children were aged 6, 3 and 1 at the time, so Christmas was expected to be busy with lots of toys and dinner with the family.

That night, before going to bed I charged the battery for the video camera so that I could record happy faces the following morning when presents were opened. I went to bed about 11.30 pm.

The phone was situated on the headboard above the bed, and at 6am it rang: it was the Control Room. One of the staff told me that a 999 call had just been received from a taxi driver who reported that, as he drove past a flat in the Old Swan area of Liverpool, the windows had blown out. It was about three miles from my home.

The taxi driver reported that flames and smoke were billowing out of the window.

I had just purchased a secondhand car to carry out my temporary promotion and it had been fitted with two-tone horns. A blue flashing light had been issued so I could stick it onto the roof while responding to emergencies. The car was a Ford Ghia – and very fast.

After the call from control I was out of bed, dressed, and in the car within two minutes and set off to the address. The roads were empty at that time on Christmas morning and I arrived within five minutes of leaving home and just as the second pump arrived at the fire.

The first machine was then based at Derby Lane Fire Station and they had arrived on the scene within two minutes of receiving the call. As I walked into the ground floor of the apartments the first crew came down the staircase carrying the body of a woman, the occupant of the flat. The woman had died due to the injuries received in the blaze. Naturally, all the crews were gutted that someone had died on Christmas Day.

The fire had to be extinguished correctly and all the burnt debris removed from the building. After a fatality at a fire, an investigation takes place. As the fire station was a hundred yards away, I suggested that I drove there, made a large pot of tea and some toast for the crews while we carried out the investigation.

When I bought the car I was only given one ignition key and hadn't had time to get a second key cut. I reached my car and put the key in the car boot to put my dirty fire tunic in there. The key snapped in two. So now I could not drive the car nor turn off the radio in the boot, which also contained my wife's Christmas present.

I am a member of the RAC *(Royal Auto Club)* and at about 7am I rang them explaining that I was a Fire Officer at an incident, I was dirty and wet, and that I couldn't get into my car because the key had snapped. I was told they would be there within an hour.

The local radio station had arrived and I was interviewed about the tragedy and asked to expand on what a terrible thing it was to happen on Christmas Day.

By 8.30am the job had been completed and the two fire engines had returned to their station but I was still waiting for the RAC. I rang them again and was told that they were having difficulty getting anyone to respond. At this time I lost all patience and asked why they advertised a 365-day service.

My brother-in-law from New Zealand, who was staying with the in-laws for Christmas, had driven down to see if he could help. But without a key the car couldn't even be towed home. By now I was the centre of interest for the neighbours, standing there in my dirty fire tunic, with a smoke-blackened face. BBC television wanted to speak to me as there had only been one fatality anywhere in the country on Christmas day.

Finally, at 10am a pickup truck appeared. The driver said that all he could do was put my car on the truck and take me home. That was all I wanted to do now, anyway. The car was manoeuvred onto the truck and I climbed into the passenger seat, just wanting to have a shower, see my kids, and apologise to my wife, as her Christmas present had been delayed.

The pickup driver then said that he had a pal who owned a garage and he had contacted him to cut some keys for the car. So off we set. It was then about 10.30 a.m. What I didn't know was that the garage was miles away up the M6 motorway. We arrived about 11.15 am and the driver's pal turned up at this little garage in the middle of nowhere.

"Oh," he said. "You didn't tell me the car was a Ford Ghia with electric windows. The doors have to come off so that I can get to the lock before cutting the keys".

I finally arrived home seven hours after leaving the house, still smelling of smoke, to find my family had abandoned their wait for me and were enjoying Christmas here, there and everywhere in my absence. I was in bed about 7.30pm on Christmas Day, totally exhausted.

The following day I had to go with a Divisional Officer to visit the relatives of the woman who had died in the fire, which was not a pleasant task but it had to be done.

We knew the fire had started in the hallway but needed to know what the heat source was and why. It appeared that the deceased used to have a clothes-drying rack in the hallway of her flat and a portable heater there to dry the wet clothes.

CHAPTER TEN

Changes of direction

Within a few weeks, my temporary promotion period was over. I returned to Toxteth Blue Watch, having enjoyed the opportunity to perform the duties of an Assistant Divisional Officer. I wanted to be successful at the next Promotion Board.

Shortly after I returned to the station, I was contacted by the Assistant Chief Fire Officer's secretary who told me that her boss wanted to see me. Off I went, thinking this may be the moment I get the nod for promotion. But no. The Assistant Chief wanted me to go around all the stations in the brigade explaining about the new pack set radios that were to be introduced following my training sessions.

So for the next few months, having received training myself first, around the stations I went, passing on the information to all the crews in the brigade.

I finished the task shortly before the next Promotion Board was about to take place. Surely this time I would be in the frame. I had done the job for nine weeks, carried out a training programme for the Assistant Chief, and felt the interview on the day had gone well.

Two weeks later I was informed that once again I had been unsuccessful. Disappointment was an understatement. Once you have been there and done the job, you want to do it all the time.

A couple of days later I received a call from a Divisional Officer friend of mine. He asked if I would be interested in a job that was available in charge of The Industrial Training Unit: it was on day shifts only. I would be the commandant in charge of providing fire training for outside organisations from all walks of life.

I decided to take the plunge. After 26 years of working shifts, I thought, "Let me see what days are like".

First of all, I had to have an interview with the Deputy Chief Fire Officer regarding my appointment. I had never met the Deputy. He had been in the Brigade for about 12 months or so, but our paths had never crossed. However his reputation went before him. Tellingly, he was generally referred to as 'The Rottweiler'.

I turned up outside the Deputy's office, where I met the Divisional Commander responsible for training, because if my application was successful, he would be my Line Manager. We were called into the Deputy's office together.

There was a very large round table in the office. The Deputy Chief sat at the far end and the Divisional Commander and I sat together at the other end. As soon as my bottom touched the seat the Deputy Chief opened up. He accused me of being lazy, someone who had finally decided to get away from the sharp end, and was looking for an easy life in training before my retirement.

The accusations were accompanied by many expletives. I had never met the man, and certainly had never been spoken to like that by a senior officer in my whole career.

I responded by asking if he usually spoke to people like that, as he had never met me before and probably knew little about me. I told him that I could sell sand to the Arabs and snow to the Eskimos.

He asked me why, in that case, I wasn't rich?

I said that the Brigade wouldn't let me do two jobs.

This really seemed to upset him and he told me to get out of his office, with expletives, discuss the Commandant's job with my wife and ring his secretary to book another appointment.

I was furious as I left his office. The Divisional Commander was visibly shaking when we got outside.

I asked: "Does the Deputy Chief always talk to everyone like that?"

"Every time," he replied.

Well I wasn't going to let that put me off. There was no way I was going to let the Deputy Chief think that his estimation of me was correct. The next morning I rang the Deputy's secretary to book another interview. The secretary asked my name. I explained who I was and she said, "You start on Monday".

I said I didn't understand and she replied briskly: "The Deputy Chief knew you wanted the job, so you start on Monday."

The following Monday I arrived at the Industrial Training Unit that was based at Banks Road in Garston. There were no courses on that day, and nothing appeared to be planned in the near future.

There were no course syllabuses, no computers, no business plan, just a typewriter that was about 30 years old.

There were two other uniformed members of staff, a Leading Fireman and Sub Officer, plus a civilian cook.

What had I let myself in for?

In the previous year the unit had made £26,000 for the Brigade that would not go halfway to covering the staff wages.

What was I supposed to bring in financially? I had not been set a target.

Time to form a plan.

I picked up the phone book and on the first day I rang several of the large factories based in Speke. Glaxo, Dista Products, Evans Medical, plus the Mersey Docks and Harbour Board, and the Mersey Tunnel Police.

I introduced myself and asked if I could visit them in my new role as Commandant of The Industrial Training Unit to discuss possible training courses. Everyone agreed to meet with me. Good start.

Over the next two weeks I met with 10 or so companies and got some firm bookings for training, particularly for company fire teams. Now it was time to go back to see the Deputy Chief. I made an appointment and went back into that office. I sat at one end of the table again and the Deputy sat at the other.

"You talk and I'll write," he said.

"Pardon?"

"You have a shopping list, so you talk and I'll write." He had read my mind and I realised at that point that it was possible we could form a good partnership.

"I need a photocopier," I said. The deputy put his hand up to stop me in mid-flow, picked the phone and rang someone.

"Mr. Fanning wants a photocopier at the Industrial Training Unit. Make sure it is there by Monday at the latest." The person at the other end must have asked where they were supposed to get a photocopier from.

"Just f****** find one, but have it there for Monday." He slammed the phone down.

My next request: "I need another cook. If I bring in more people, there will be a need to provide more meals." The same routine followed: the phone was picked up, a number dialled and someone was ordered to finance another cook. Again they dared to query the order and were choked off with another volley of expletives and ordered to get it done now.

I went through everything I needed, including more staff. I was told I could hand-pick my staff from anyone in the Brigade. If they needed to be promoted that would be done, but if I got it wrong my head would be on the chopping block.

At the end of the session the Deputy told me to go away, not to break the law, but make as much money as I could for the Brigade.

Earning money for the Fire Service

So began the three-year cycle that started in 1992. I set a target of £80,000 in year one and we smashed it; £100,000 in year two and we smashed that; and at the end of year three we had turned over £250,000.

We landed large contracts with Evans Medical, Glaxo, Mersey Tunnel Police, and Her Majesty's Customs and Excise.

I had new equipment specially constructed for training the Tunnel Police. A friend of mine welded steel frames together in the shape of a vehicle so we could start a fire inside the equipment and use it over and over again. Old cars burnt out too quickly and were costly to purchase.

We also had two 40-foot containers designed inside with staircases and hatches to train Mersey Docks tug boat crews in dealing with fires at sea.

My staff was brilliant and all the customers enjoyed their firefighting or breathing apparatus training experiences. We built up a reputation, and now companies were ringing us for training, not us ringing them.

I was there for three years and really enjoyed being the boss of a business. The Brigade sent me on a finance course where I had learnt a lot and it came in really useful when I was working out budgets and planning the year ahead. We particularly enjoyed working with the men and women of Customs and Excise. After a few months of delivering training to the first few courses they decided to send all their training to us at Banks Road.

H.M. Customs had commandeered a vessel that they had apprehended in the English Channel loaded with false decks and millions of pounds worth of drugs. The engine was removed and the bowels of the vessel were used to train the Customs staff wearing breathing apparatus to search for contraband, money or illegal immigrants.

Once the training session started, we would sound the distress alarm of one of the trainees and tell them to lie down and await rescue. The rescue team would have to don an air-line, make their way down to find their colleague and carry out the rescue.

We would spend all day aboard the vessel taking a packed lunch and flasks with us, returning to Banks Road to debrief after the training session. The course lasted three days and we used to get great feedback from everyone who attended.

Then we had one-day firefighting courses for Fire Wardens from all types of workplaces. The women who attended enjoyed getting dressed up in the fire kit and helmets to tackle the chip pans or small oil fires we used to light to practice use of fire extinguishers. A few days after a course we would receive thank you cards and occasionally cakes or chocolates.

Sometimes, when I was off-duty in Liverpool city centre, someone would come up to me and ask if I remembered them from one of our courses. They told me how much they had enjoyed the experience.

Lots of interest was being shown in the training we were providing and courses would fill up very quickly. Everything was going very well and the money kept coming in.

A derelict bus has an unexpected end

When I had arrived to start my role as the Training Commandant, there had been an old single-decker bus parked in the yard. It had been used many years ago to simulate rescuing passengers off an aircraft. The vehicle had been vandalised, its windows smashed and tyres punctured. I decided that the bus needed to be removed from the site as it was an eyesore. Once gone there would be additional parking for people attending our training courses.

One morning I told one of my Leading Fireman that I was off to the main training centre for a daylong meeting, and asked him to ring around to see if any scrap dealers were interested in picking up the bus.

When I returned later that afternoon I was informed that someone was coming from Yorkshire to pick up the bus and was going to bring £600 payment with him. I went into a blind panic and immediately sought clarification: "Does he know the bus is wrecked and the tyres flat?" I was assured that the dealer was aware of the state of the vehicle.

I sat in the office thinking that some very large muscular scrap dealer was about to storm in and rant about coming all the way from Yorkshire for that pile of rubbish. Shortly afterwards I could hear the sound of a heavy vehicle entering the yard. Strangely enough, all my trusted instructors had decided to keep out of the way. A few minutes passed and there was a knock on my door and a large gentleman in a vest and baggy trousers entered.

"I've come to pick up t' bus," he declared.

"Have you seen it? Is it all right for you?" I asked, fearing the answer.

"Oh aye, it's grand. All that aluminium is worth a few bob and some of the seats are in good order. I can make a tidy profit." With that he chucked £600 in £20 notes on the desk and asked for a receipt, which I swiftly produced. Off he went, and I heaved a large sigh of relief. The following day I took the money down to the finance department. As usual, nothing was easy. There were questions asked: Where did the money come from? How did the dealer know about the vehicle? Who gave me permission to sell the bus?

I suggested they contact the Deputy Chief Fire Officer if they had a problem. Once I mentioned the Deputy Chief, the money was accepted without further question. I was given a receipt and, as I drove back to Banks Road, I thought it hadn't been such a bad day: we had banked an extra £600 that we hadn't planned on.

CHAPTER ELEVEN

Firefighting training for refugee ships

One afternoon the telephone rang and it was a local shipping company asking if I would like to quote for providing breathing apparatus training for British seaman in the port of Hamburg, in Germany.

I wasn't sure how to quote for such a course, so spoke to my immediate Line Manager who said I was to cost it out on two officers' pay for three days with all other expenses being paid by the shipping company. I provided a quote and within a very short time it was accepted.

Now I have to admit I do not like flying, and so I was going to send the two Sub Officers who were on my team to carry out the training. But my Line Manager said that, as the Commandant, I would have to go to oversee the training.

I had been told that we would be providing training for British seamen who were manning ships containing refugees from the war in Bosnia.

The Liverpool Echo picked up on the story and my the Sub Officer and I were duly photographed, and appeared as local firefighters travelling to Germany to assist British seamen looking after war-torn refugees. Radio Merseyside also interviewed us before we left for Germany.

One of my Sub Officers, Dave Perrin, had been attending German language courses run by the Fire Brigade, so he was a natural to take with me.

Imagine my disappointment when we boarded a Lufthansa flight at Manchester Airport and the very attractive flight attendant greeted me with *'Guten Abend'* to which I responded, but when we sat in our seats, Dave asked me what *'Guten Abend'* meant.

The last time I had been in an aircraft was over 35 years earlier and I was very nervous. Dave and I were in uniform. The two flight attendants said how much they liked firemen in uniform and that they would look after us on the flight.

The plane took off and I was like the guy in the film 'Airplane' who sweats profusely. Every time the plane moved slightly, I turned to Dave and asked what was going on. At first he thought it was a prank but slowly it dawned on him that I didn't like flying at all.

After what seemed hours we landed in Hamburg and I immediately realised that in three days I would have to fly back and go through all that panic again.

We arrived at a very nice hotel in Hamburg, had a meal and turned in for the night. There had been no contact from anyone when we arrived at the hotel, so in the morning we had breakfast and waited around. About an hour later the phone rang in our room and an angry person wanted to know why we had not arrived at the ship as arranged.

I explained that we had not been given instructions on what to do after our arrival. It appeared that the hotel staff had failed to give me details that had been forwarded for our attention.

A taxi was quickly called and we set off on our journey. I told the taxi driver the name of the 'ship' in Hamburg docks and Dave and I sat in the back of the taxi. The driver did not move. I repeated the address to which the driver said, *"Nein."* Now, even with my limited German I knew this meant "No", so I repeated the address and got the same response, *"Nein."*

Panic began to set in as we were already late to start the training. We were in uniform, so in my broken German I tried to explain what we were going to do if and when he took us to the docks. Slowly the taxi began to move forwards and we set off. However the driver kept looking in his driving mirror and shaking his head.

As we drove into the docks we realised why he was reluctant to transport us. There in front of us were row after row of vessels, mostly constructed of rusting metal containers, some as high as a six-storey building.

Lots of people who were obviously from other lands were milling about.

The driver said he was not going to stop and motioned to me to throw the money on the front seat as he slowed down.

Dave and I had to jump out while the vehicle was moving.

We looked for the name of the vessel we were meant to be visiting and eventually found it. There was a guard armed with a rifle standing on the gangplank stopping anyone from entering or leaving the vessel.

I approached him and asked to be taken to see the captain. He motioned to follow him and we walked up a flight of stairs and stopped outside a cabin. The armed guard knocked on the door which was then unlocked and we were ushered inside. The captain greeted us and asked us to sit down in the cabin.

We both obviously looked shocked so the captain filled us in with the details of what was going on.

On this particular vessel there were 960 refugees, it seemed from all over the world. They were all seeking asylum in Germany. There were people from different religions and different tribes from the same country, some of these were ancient enemies. Fights were a regular occurrence.

Some of the refugees had never used cookers before, so a kitchen fire was also a common occurrence.

In the beginning the German fire brigade had attended promptly. But, as fire calls to this and to others of the dozen vessels tied up in Hamburg harbour became so frequent, the German authorities told the vessel owners that they could only call for assistance after 15 minutes if the crew could not deal with the fire.

That was the reason for our visit. The crew had not worn breathing apparatus for many years and obviously they would need it to tackle fires inside one of the many containers on the vessel.

What we had to do was to teach them how to don and start the breathing apparatus sets provided by the shipping company, and how to search in a smoke-filled room.

To do the training we used the captain's cabin. We blanked out the visors on the breathing apparatus and watched the crew search for either me or Dave as we lay on the floor under a table or under a bunk. By making a few minor adjustments or moving bits of furniture we changed the layout of the cabin to give the crew more scenarios to deal with.

The crew were good lads and very keen to learn because they could be at real risk in the event of a serious fire.

After a few hours of training, the captain gave us a tour of the vessel. It was like nothing I had ever seen before it all my years in the fire brigade.

In the containers, as far as the eye could see were bunk beds with lots of refugees lying in them. There was lots of half-eaten food, and sandwiches and meat strewn all over the floor.

There was vomit.

There were clothes lines hanging from the series of bunk beds with cockroaches walking across the lines.

The sight reminded me very much of the original series of 'Roots' when overcrowded boats of African slaves were being transported across the seas to America.

It was very difficult to take in what the four crew members on this vessel had to deal with, having 960 people crowded aboard in such conditions.

The next day we visited the smaller vessel next door, which had 300 people on board and just two crew members. It was bad, but slightly better than that of the previous day.

Upon our return to Liverpool we were interviewed again by Radio Merseyside. Before the reporter began with her questions, off air, I said to her: "When we are on live interview please do not ask me any questions about conditions on the vessels".

The interview lasted for a few minutes and just as it was about to finish the reporter asked me what conditions were like on board, to which I replied, "No comment".

The interview finished and then we spoke about what we had seen over the three days in Hamburg. Obviously after a story, the reporter rang the shipping line for a comment. The shipping line then rang me, very angrily denying that conditions were like that in Germany.

My response to them was I had no idea what the British crew members were being paid to serve on the vessels but it was nowhere near enough for what they had to put up with.

Needless to say the shipping company decided not to use our services again as there had been plans to do similar training in Scandinavia for crewmen looking after refugees there.

Creating a 'boil over'

During our one-day fire training sessions we held at the Industrial Training Unit, we always showed the people on the course a 'boil over'. This was where we put a container of water into a boiling drum of oil simulating the results of putting water on to a chip pan fire.

The staff used to try and make the boil over as spectacular as possible and to outdo each other with height of the flames and the pall of smoke. Before we did the demonstration though, we always had to warn Liverpool Airport in case an approaching aircraft thought a crash had occurred.

Back to the beginning

One day when the phone rang, it was the Deputy Chief. He invited me to his office, where he said he thought I deserved a promotion for the good job I had done over the last three years.

I thanked him and said I really liked what I was doing and wanted to stay where I was.

He said that I misunderstood. I didn't have any choice in the matter. He had another job lined up for me as a temporary Assistant Divisional Officer Station Commander.

Reluctantly I agreed. You didn't argue with the Deputy. "Okay where do you want me to go?"

"I want you to go back to Toxteth. You seem to be able to get on with everyone there." I was taken aback and not expecting to see Toxteth with all its unique issues again.

"Can have I free rein to get into the schools and attempt to prevent the young kids becoming the stone-throwers and fire-lighters of the future?" I asked.

"You are the Station Commander. It is your area, your responsibility to do what you can to reduce incidents of all kinds, so get on with it." That was his parting shot.

So, in 1995, I returned to Toxteth Fire Station.

My office was a Portakabin in the station yard.

I was ready for the unexpected as usual and I wasn't disappointed.

CHAPTER TWELVE

Station Commander Duties

As a Station Commander you worked an 84-hour week. You had to do so many hours office duty on days, and you were on call from home for the rest of the hours you had to work. The worst period to provide cover was from 9am on Friday morning, until 9am on Monday morning.

Sometimes, there would be two Assistant Divisional Officers *(ADOs)* and a Divisional Officer *(DO)* covering our particular zone, but often there would only be one ADO. The zone we covered included Toxteth, the city centre, and sometimes the Wirral on the other side of the River Mersey.

My nightmare was to turn out to the Wirral. Bear in mind that this was before Sat Nav, so if a house fire occurred, a traffic accident, or other incident, when the telephone rang I had to make my way to what was affectionately called the 'Dark Side'. We were all unfamiliar with that area in contrast to our local one.

I would put on the two-tone horns and set off on the four miles to the Mersey tunnels. The tunnel police would pick me up on the CCTV cameras racing through and open one of the barriers to ease my trip. Unfortunately I had to stop the car after I had cleared the tunnel and get out my route finder so I could locate the destination address.

Most nights when I was on duty I would climb into bed about 11pm and it would be unusual if I wasn't disturbed at least twice during the night.

I provided my own car, which was now a red Volvo saloon into which the Brigade fitted two-tone horns and a hands-free radio. Having attended an Emergency Drivers' Course, I would have to speed off into the night to reach whatever incident had occurred. The worst times were during the winter months – leaving a warm bed, dressing quickly, and then jumping into a freezing car with a frozen windscreen, spraying the screen to defrost, setting off on icy roads, and arriving at the incident. Then I had to get my freezing cold fire kit and boots from the boot of the car, dress, and then take charge of the incident with a clear head.

One early morning in 1995, I set off to attend a house fire in Toxteth. Traffic was light and I was travelling at a good pace. As I made my way down Mulgrave Street at speed, a car overtook my vehicle and swerved across the road, forcing me to stop. Instantly, another car pulled in behind me. Two men in balaclavas jumped out of the front car and started to walk towards my vehicle.

I always carried my fire helmet on the front seat of the car. For some unknown reason I picked it up as I got out of the car, put it on and asked what was going on.

"Sorry man," was the response from one of the men in a balaclava. "We thought you was the law."

Both cars then raced off and I rather gingerly made my way to the incident.

Mulgrave Street is a diagonal cut-through between two main arterial roads and not very long. The men must have been waiting to set the trap.

I sent a memo the next day to all officers that may attend an incident in Toxteth in my absence, to ensure there was some way of indicating in your vehicle that you were a fire officer and not a police officer on the way to an incident.

Such incidents were few and far between, but it was important to get across to the community that we were there to help, in that respect it was important to try and distance ourselves from the police in Toxteth.

Initiating a community solution

I decided that the time was right to implement my idea to go into the local primary schools in the Toxteth area and tell the young children what we did as firefighters; about the danger of playing with matches and lighters; and to ask them not to throw stones at us, and not to make hoax calls.

I wrote to the Head Teachers of all 26 primary schools in our station area, offering them a firefighter for their school and explaining that their firefighter would go into the school and talk to the children about fire safety and tell them what their job entailed. I received 17 positive responses. Now I had to get four volunteers from the four Watches to get the idea off the ground. I had expected a bit of apprehension but there wasn't a problem.

The idea was that the firefighters would have about four schools each they would visit during their day shifts, after making arrangements with the Head Teacher.

The four volunteers enjoyed it so much that two of them used to go into the schools on their days off. They got invited to school prize days, school plays, and assemblies. At Christmas they would receive Christmas cards from the classes they had spoken to during the school term.

After 12 months I decided to take the idea a bit further. I had been asked to join the Toxteth Crime Prevention Panel and had attended a number of meetings.

At the next meeting, I asked if there was any way they could provide funding for miniature fire tunics and helmets for the school children to wear when the safety talks took place.

There was a lady from Barclays Bank who was a member of the Panel, and she agreed to ask the bank to fund the initiative, which they did.

The idea had taken off and other fire brigades started to ring me and ask how I had got the scheme started. The last bridge to cross was the largest secondary school in the station area.

I wanted to arrange leadership training, again with the help of volunteers from the station, and then to send a number of girls and boys to the Industrial Training Unit for a full day's fire training.

Once they had successfully completed the day, right there at the Unit they would receive a certificate for their CVs.

The problem at the school was that the majority of the school children were from families who had immigrated recently to England from countries far less well off than ours.

They felt that because of their skin colour and where they lived, the chances of them getting employment were negligible. They would say: "Why should they go to university?"

Guys who had left the school a year or two ago were now driving BMWs and that was what they wanted to do. I had a black firefighter on one of the watches and he agreed to talk in the training sessions. When the kids said they wouldn't get jobs, my firefighter would say: "I got a job, and I am black." When they said their friends were driving expensive cars and wearing designer clothes, he would say that in next to no time they would be in jail or dead because they were involved in drug dealing and that was not the way to go.

Again the scheme began to bear fruit and all the boys and girls particularly enjoyed the firefighting sessions.

Royal recognition

The Crime Prevention Panel members were pleased with the progress we were making and entered the scheme into a competition. A few months later I received a letter telling us that we had won two 'Business in The Community' Awards.

We had to travel to London and receive the awards from H.R.H. Prince Charles. Together with three of my community firefighters, we travelled to London in a Fire Brigade vehicle that looked as if it had been used for stock car racing.

We were put up in a very plush hotel overnight.

The Chief Fire Officer had travelled to London by train to attend the ceremony. The Chief contacted me and asked for me and the three firefighters to meet him, which we did. He took us all out on the town to a restaurant for a meal and beers.

We were a bit embarrassed and decided that we should put £10 each in to a kitty and invite the Chief to have a drink at our expense. What followed was a bit of a pub-crawl led by the Chief before we arrived back at the hotel rather late.

Next morning after breakfast we changed into our uniforms to make our way to Lancaster House where the award ceremony was to take place. We met the Chief Fire Officer at the front of the hotel and he joined us in the battered brigade vehicle for the drive to the ceremony.

We arrived at Lancaster House about 30 minutes before the ceremony was to start. At the gate we were met and saluted by a police officer in a blue box very like Doctor Who's Tardis. He checked our ID and waved us through, but as we drove into the yard a man in uniform ran in front of the car and asked us what we thought we were doing. I explained we had an appointment with H.R.H. Prince Charles in 25 minutes.

"Well you can't park here. Nelson Mandela is in town and there's no parking allowed at Lancaster House today".

Not being familiar with nearby London parking arrangements, I left the car and walked back to the policeman on the gate. He threw me another salute as I approached him, "Yes sir, what's the problem?" he asked.

"We can't park here due to security for Nelson Mandela, and we have to meet H.R.H. Prince Charles in 20 minutes," I explained.

The policeman picked up the receiver on a very old looking telephone in his box and wound up a handle on the side of the phone. He spoke to whoever answered the phone and explained our predicament. When he had finished he gave me instructions.

"Tell your driver, sir, to drive down the Mall. One of my colleagues will stop your vehicle and show him where to park. If he comes through the Queen Mother's back garden over there, you should be in time for your appointment".

I went back to the car and spoke to Barry Johnson, the driver, explaining what to do and asked if he minded following the instructions. No problem. So everyone else got out of the car and we stood and waited for Barry to return. Ten minutes later Barry returned with a big grin on his face.

"Boss, that was great," Barry said. "The Mall is closed to all vehicles, so there I was driving down the empty road when an armed policeman stopped the car and indicated to follow him.

"All down The Mall shining black Mercedes were parked on the verges, with the drivers all dressed in grey suits and sunglasses. I parked our tatty red Fire Brigade vehicle next to them. Fantastic". Barry will remember that experience for the rest of his life.

We made our way into Lancaster House, which was stunning inside, and were directed to a large function room for the ceremony.

Sitting on the row in front of us was Sir Trevor McDonald, the television celebrity newsreader, and other dignitaries. Prince Charles came in and delivered a short speech congratulating all the award winners.

I had decided that as the Chief Fire Officer was present he should collect the award on behalf of Merseyside Fire Brigade, so instead of me shaking hands with H.R.H. on a big photograph it was the Chief.

Refreshments were served afterwards and we mingled with the dignitaries.

A woman approached me and said: "You should be very proud of your men. They look very smart in their uniforms."

I thanked her and said I was very proud because they had brought my plans for children's fire education to fruition and it was they who had really won the award.

We were wearing name badges but the dignitaries were not. I apologised to the woman that I didn't know her name to address her personally.

"I am Lady Howe, Sir Geoffrey's wife," she replied.

Sir Geoffrey Howe was the longest serving Cabinet minister in Margaret Thatcher's government, holding held the posts of Chancellor of the Exchequer, Foreign Secretary, and Leader of the House of Commons, later to be Deputy Prime Minister and President of the Council.

We left the Chief Fire Officer at the ceremony and set off back to Liverpool in the battered red fire brigade car, full of stories to tell when we returned to our duties next time.

As well as the community firefighters visiting their schools, we arranged a yearly painting competition for all of the schools that had agreed to join the scheme.

Once again Barclays Bank and the Crime Prevention Panel agreed to fund the prize-giving day by providing trophies and covering the catering costs for the sandwiches and cakes provided for the prizewinners and the schoolteachers that attended.

In the photo on the next page, I am looking down from the fire engine on the little girl with the trophy she won for the painting competition

The first year we held the prize-giving a Senior Divisional Officer attended, and after four years the Chief Fire Officer finally made an appearance.

After presenting the prizes, the Chief Fire Officer praised the idea and said it was exactly what he thought the Brigade should be doing.

The day after I retired, the same Chief Officer cancelled the scheme.

CHAPTER THIRTEEN

The need for fire station security

As previously mentioned, when I went back to Toxteth as the Station Commander, my office was a Portakabin in the station yard: lovely in the summer months, but freezing in the winter.

The year after I arrived we had a visit from the H.M.I. *(Her Majesty's Inspectorate of Fire Brigades).* When the inspectors came to the Brigade everyone was told to ensure that stations and the machines were gleaming and, if asked to perform a drill, that it was to be done to the highest standard.

On the day the inspector was due to inspect our station, I was in my Portakabin and I heard the loudspeaker system operate. Both the pump and the turntable ladder turned out to a fire.

Five minutes later a fleet of cars drove into the yard. Senior officers always escorted the H.M.I., in case anyone spoke out of turn, or performed abysmally.

I was sitting at my desk when the H.M.I. walked through the doorway.

"Are you the Station Commander?" was the question fired at me.

I replied that I was, stood to attention and saluted the Inspector.

"Your fire station looks like Fort Apache in the Bronx, with all the razor wire around the walls and the gates locked."

I responded by explaining that if we didn't have the razor wire and lock the station gates every time the machines turned out and the station was empty, there would be nothing left when we returned.

The Inspector looked at me with incredulity, obviously not believing what I was saying. I decided to give him a recent example.

"Two weeks ago Green Watch from this station turned out to a local Public House on fire. The landlord's dog was trapped on the upper floor by the blaze. Two firefighters in breathing apparatus rescued the dog, which was unconscious, and carried it into the street, where the remaining members of the crew gave the dog oxygen and revived it.

"Unfortunately, while everyone's attention was focused on saving the animal, a couple of members of the society that we serve opened one of the lockers on the machine and stole a number of items of gear.

Last week I received a phone call from a police officer in Newton Abbot, Devon, some four and half hours away, asking if I could identify a crowbar with 'S6 High Park Street' on it.

I responded in the affirmative: it was from my station, and it was stolen the previous week. The police officer said that the crowbar had been used on a robbery."

When I finished the story the Inspector's mouth fell open and he swung round to address the Assistant Chief Officer who was in the escort party.

"Why don't we at the Home Office know about incidents like this", he demanded.

It was obvious from this 10-minute incident that certainly the Home Office and probably the majority of Senior Officers in Merseyside Brigade had no idea what was happening, not just on the fire ground but when the fire stations were unoccupied.

A vacated station provided an ideal time for unauthorised persons to gain access and steal anything they could get their hands on. The Blue Watch mess-tin was returned to the station by someone from a nearby block of apartments who had discovered it tossed aside there: it was empty, of course.

Firefighters' cars were often vandalised in the station yard, so eventually, if one of the engine-house bays were empty, permission was given to park personal vehicles inside during night duty.

There were some scallywags in the local community, but the vast majority of the people we served appreciated the fact that we looked after them when they needed our assistance.

Honouring former firefighters

One memorable event I remember happened in 1996. At Christmas time the Fire Service Benevolent Fund used to provide presents for retired firefighters known to the organisation. Accordingly, one of my responsibilities was to deliver the presents to any ex-colleagues living in my station area.

One pensioner lived very close to the station and I drove to the street to deliver the gift. I parked the car but before I could reach the front door the old guy was standing there asking if I was looking for him.

I gave him the gift and wished him Merry Christmas and returned to the station.

Some months later a young woman called at the station and asked to speak to the Station Commander. She was shown to my office and I asked how I could help.

The woman explained that in two weeks' time her grandfather, who had served in the fire service during the war, would be celebrating being been married for 60 years. She asked if I could present him with something from Merseyside Fire Brigade, congratulating him on the event. When I asked the address, it turned out to be the man I had met delivering the gift at Christmas.

I said I would do what I could and to leave it with me. A pal of mine worked at Brigade HQ as the press liaison officer, so I asked for his help in producing some kind of memento with a fire brigade theme.

A couple of days later I went back to HQ and took delivery of some very striking art work on parchment. It was decorated with silver axes and hose branches. The message on the document read:

Congratulations from Merseyside Fire Brigade
(and here the names of the man and his wife)
on celebrating 60 years of marriage.

The following day I contacted the couple's granddaughter and asked when it would be convenient to deliver the framed certificate.

A few hours later I called round to find most of the couple's children, grand and great grandchildren gathered in the very small Victorian era terraced house the couple shared off High Park Street, a few blocks away from the more elegant houses that edged Princes Park.

I presented the gentleman with the certificate, which he read and then became very emotional. He said they had received a letter of congratulations from the Queen but that this framed certificate from the fire brigade meant so much to him. As he shook my hand when I went to leave, I asked if I could call round and see him the following week for a chat. We arranged a date and time for our meeting.

A week or so later I met up with the gentleman and, over a cup of tea, he told me of some incredible experiences he had encountered during his time in the Auxiliary Fire Service during the war in Liverpool.

The man was a painter and decorator by trade when the war broke out. He wanted to join the army but was only four foot eleven in height and told he couldn't fight, so he joined the AFS.

He was stationed in the dock area and the firemen used to supply the dockers with tea, sugar and milk while they were loading and unloading the cargos that were so vital to keeping the country going during the war.

The deliveries were made by bicycle. One night his job was to take the supplies to the dock hut, and off he set. Just after he started his journey, the air-raid warning sounded. He decided to carry on and join the dockers in the nearest air-raid shelter while the raid was on.

He said he had turned into the dock avenue where the hut was just as a German plane flew overhead. It dropped its bombs, scoring a direct hit on the hut. He was knocked off his bicycle by the blast wave.

I asked what he did next, and he said he jumped on his bicycle and rode back to the fire station because the dockers wouldn't be needing the supplies after all.

Another tale he told was how during firefighting operations at a large blaze he was positioned on one of the walls with a colleague, directing water onto the burning inferno of the building's interior.

On one of the opposite walls were five other firemen directing their hoses below. Suddenly, the wall opposite collapsed and the firemen plunged into the inferno below. He never saw them again.

The hour or so I spent with this man reminded me of the tales my Uncle George used to tell during my childhood.

Life expectancy for firefighters during the Blitz was extremely short and they were all heroes, whether fighting fires in Liverpool or in the other cities they were directed to when the Luftwaffe decided to switch their bombing attack to other targets.

After the war finished, my storyteller wanted to stay in the fire service, but because of his profession and the need for homes to be rebuilt, painted and decorated, he was denied the opportunity.

I contacted the brigade historian after my visit and suggested he should contact the man and listen to his tales. A few weeks later the man's wife died, then months later he too passed away. I was on leave when he died. His daughter called at the station to tell me of his death.

The station officer who was on duty realised the significance and, when the man's funeral took place, the fire engine and crew from Toxteth attended the church, a gesture greatly appreciated by the whole family.

Issues of life and death not related to fire fighting

They say that life is full of experiences both good and bad. The beauty of mine is that I have experienced just about everything that life can throw at you. Because of that background I found it quite easy to deal with the problems that often landed at my office door.

Firefighters would come in and tell me their problems and their worries and I could point them in a certain direction, as I had had to deal with a similar problem in my operational or personal life.

Divorce? Been there.

Death of loved ones, serious illness, shortage of money. I had dealt with all of these, often with great difficulty, but I had come through it, and I passed on to my firefighters how I had managed the problems that rocked my life.

One time that hit me hard was an event that it proved very, very few officers had ever experienced.

I was fast asleep in bed off-duty when the phone rang. It was 2am. Sleepy-eyed I picked up the receiver. In the background I could hear the noise of the staff in the fire brigade control room. I thought at first they had rung me in error thinking I was on duty, then a voice said, "Mr. Fanning, I am sorry to bother you but we thought you ought to know that one of your firefighters has gone missing."

I sat bolt upright, now wide-awake. What did they mean? The control room operator carried on, "The police have contacted us and said they are concerned for the firefighter's safety."

I asked for the identity of the missing person and was given the name of a young man who had been in Merseyside Fire Brigade for less than 18 months: a nice lad, bubbly personality, enthusiastic, hardworking.

Surely there must be some mistake.

The operator asked if they could contact me again if they received any further information.

I lay in bed, my mind was whirling. What was going on? Surely there was a mistake.

I must have drifted back to sleep to be woken again about 6am. I grabbed the phone. It was the same operator: "Mr. Fanning, I am sorry to inform you that Merseyside Police have been in contact with us. Your firefighter has been killed by a train in Garston."

In all the courses I had attended in my career – officers' courses, management courses at the Fire Service College – not one of those had ever explained what an Officer in Charge should do when one of his staff commits suicide.

I got out of bed, showered and then sat and waited at home until the office staff was due into Brigade HQ. Then I rang to ask for advice on what I should do now.

I was told to go and see the parents. I asked, "What should I say?" The answer could be paraphrased as: "Make it up. You are on your own. There is nothing written down advising the best course of action in such circumstances".

I drove to Runcorn where the firefighter's parents lived. Runcorn is another cargo port on the River Mersey. It is in Cheshire on the other side of the river from Liverpool. The drive took about 50 minutes, and all the way I was going through what I might say when I arrived.

I thought I would walk up the path, knock on the door, introduce myself, offer my condolences and take it from there.

I was in uniform of course and as I pulled up outside the house, before I had even stopped the engine, the man's father was standing by the driver's door.

I got out of the car and the man grabbed my hand, shaking it and thanking me for coming so quickly. It threw me off my intended course of action and I followed him up the path into the house.

The firefighter's mother was sitting in the living room as I entered. I was immediately drawn to the number of photographs in the room on the walls and on every available flat surface.

The parents had three children: there was an older brother and his photograph was there with his children; an older sister and her photograph was there with her children; and every other picture was of our firefighter. He was there in his football kit, running gear, university gown, firefighting gear – everywhere in that house he was there.

I started by saying I had only known their son for 18 months or so but he was going the right way, good at his duties on the station and also on the fire ground. I had to give him practical tests out on the drill ground every six months or so and rate his performance. He never had any problems.

The father made me a cup of tea and I finally sat down, still feeling out of my depth in this situation.

The mother then told me about her son and it was as if I had known a different person.

It appeared that the reason he had taken his life was following a £500 bet on two football matches the previous night. Checking what that would be worth in 2019 shows that it was the equivalent today of £2,126.

Manchester United were playing at Old Trafford and Liverpool were playing somewhere in Europe. Manchester United had been winning 3-0 at half time but drew 3-3 and Liverpool had drawn 0-0. He had lost on both bets.

I like a bet on horses and football but never bet more than I can afford to lose. I found it hard to believe that a young firefighter with his whole life in front of him had ended it over a losing football bet.

Driving back to the station from Runcorn that morning, I decided that I was going to speak to every Watch on the station and ask every firefighter to come and see me if they had any problems, either in work or outside work. I never wanted to face this situation again.

There was another occasion when I received a disturbing phone call from the control room. I was on the worst shift a Station Commander had to cover, which was that from 9am on a Friday morning to 9am on the following Monday morning.

At about 7.30am on the Monday morning, after what had been a fairly quiet couple of nights, I received a call from the control room. The operator said there had been a death on the fire station at Canning Place. Once again it didn't sink in at first and I thought that they meant that someone had been found dead who had been sleeping rough at the back of the station, as often happened. No: it was one of the Watch.

Driving to the fire station, I knew quite a few of the guys there and I was hoping desperately that it wasn't someone that I knew personally who had died.

On arrival, I was met by the officer in charge and we went into his office. He explained that at 7am most of the guys were up and tidying the station and a few were still in the night room. They shouted to a colleague who was still in bed to 'rise and shine'. When there was no response, they approached the bed and saw immediately that their colleague was dead. Via the Control Room, I requested the police to attend, as this was a sudden death.

By this time it was about 8.30 and the Night Watch were going off duty and were due back at 6pm that night.

I told the officer in charge to get the crew together and ask if anyone didn't feel up to coming back that night due to the death of their colleague. Every one of them said they were prepared to return for night duty: they wanted to stick together.

By this time the Assistant Chief Fire Officer had arrived on the station and I briefed him on the background and told him where we were up to. Shortly afterwards, the Chief Fire Officer rang and spoke with me with regards to informing the Station Commander for Canning Place who was not due in for duty until the following day.

I rang the Station Commander and he asked me to arrange with the Station Officer to collect the firefighter's personal belongings and store them for the next of kin. I finally left the station at about 11.30am when the body had been removed and the police had spoken to the officer in charge. I went home fatigued after what had been another unhappy occurrence, looking forward to my two days off before returning on Wednesday.

On the Wednesday morning the office phone rang and it was my pal the Station Commander from Canning Place. He thanked me for my efforts on Monday morning and thought I might like to know what had happened since. When the watch at Canning Place returned to duty on the Monday night, the Station Officer and another one of the ranks unlocked the deceased firefighter's locker to put his personal items in bags for the next of kin.

About 7pm the Station Officer rang the Station Commander to say that when they were emptying the locker they had found some cannabis. The Station Commander had said to throw it in the waste bin, to which the station officer replied: "I cannot lift it." At this, the Station Commander told the Station Officer to lock the locker and call the police immediately.

Within 20 minutes or so there were sniffer dogs and police officers all over the station.

The immediate thought was that the firefighter's death may have been caused by drugs; however, following an inquest, it proved that the cause of death was a heart attack.

Nobody knew why there were drugs in the locker, nor their planned destination.

CHAPTER FOURTEEN

The blonde on a ledge in her negligée

The surprises and the unusual calls kept coming thick and fast.

One night, I was deep asleep, but on call, when the phone rang. Control informed me that they had turned the crew from Toxteth out to a call from a member of the public who could see a woman screaming on a ledge about 40 feet above the ground.

Quickly I dressed, jumped into the car and drove off to the incident. When I arrived an ambulance was just leaving the scene and I feared the worst as there had been a couple of suicides in the area over the past few years by people jumping off the roof of a multi-storey block. Fortunately, I had missed attending those.

The officer charge informed me that when he arrived there was a young blonde woman in a negligée screaming atop a ledge about three floors above the ground.

Because of the woman's obvious distress the officer decided it was safer to send for the hydraulic platform appliance rather than pitch a ladder and send a firefighter up to help the woman down.

The hydraulic platform had arrived and brought the woman down without any problem.

It transpired that the woman had been in a flat on the upper floor with a man. They had an argument and the man punched her in the face.

She fled, climbing out of the window onto the ledge screaming for help. The man had then run off.

The officer said that the woman had a bleeding nose but no serious injuries. Everyone returned to their station and I went back home to bed.

Two nights later, I was off duty and went for a pint to my local hostelry. While I was there a pal of mine who was a police officer in Toxteth, also off duty, arrived for a beer. I began to tell him the story of the blonde in the negligée on the ledge and the way she had been rescued.

My pal continued sipping his beer and appeared not to be listening, so I asked him had he heard about this from one of the Bobbies at the station. He turned to me and whispered, "I didn't tell you this, but that woman is HIV and a Hepatitis B carrier."

Right. So now I did have a problem.

Some of the firefighters may have come into contact with this lady when she was bleeding. A day later when the watch came back on duty I went on parade and asked a series of questions.

Question One: At the incident with the lady on the ledge did any of you physically touch her?

Now, normally when the hydraulic platform arrives at an incident, it takes a few minutes to set up. The vehicle has to be jacked up so the wheels come off the road. Then one firefighter gets into the cage fitted on the extending booms to assist the person who needs to be rescued.

Because this was a blonde in a negligée, five firemen got into the cage for a closer look.

Question Two: Did anyone get any of the lady's blood on their clothing?

Two firefighters' hands went up. I told them to remove the clothing and put the contaminated garments into the soluble bags we carried on the fire engine and seal them.

Question Three: Did anyone else touch this woman?

The driver's hand went up.

I was puzzled and asked, "How did you come to touch her?"

"Well Boss," came the reply, "When we got the young woman down from the ledge, she insisted on giving us all a kiss."

Now I have got some very worried faces looking at me.

"What's this all about," one of the crew asked.

I told them the full story and a couple of them went white and started asking what are we going to do.

I rang the control room and put the fire engine off the run.

I then rang the Brigade Driving School and requested a mini-bus to transport the crew into Liverpool city centre for advice and counselling regarding HIV and possible infection.

Following that, I called the Royal Liverpool Hospital to arrange for the contaminated clothing to be cleaned to remove any possibility of the HIV or Hepatitis virus remaining.

After visiting the Advice Centre, four of the crew were advised to have blood tests, which fortunately proved that they had not contracted either of the viruses.

Firefighting among drug use remains

Due to the nature of area in which we worked, the majority of the crews had been vaccinated against Hepatitis B. They would often enter burning buildings to tackle fires and after the blaze was extinguished they would discover discarded syringes and other drug paraphernalia.

Occasionally they would crawl over syringes or human faeces, and as the drug users may have had Hepatitis B it was obviously better to take the precaution of having a course of injections.

I particularly remember attending a blaze in a disused warehouse in Duke Street in the city centre, where it was known that people slept rough and often took drugs.

Smoke was pouring out of an open doorway and teams of firefighters wearing breathing apparatus were waiting to enter to tackle the fire.

One of the first crews into the warehouse exited carrying an old car tyre, which had a number of syringes stuck in it.

The car tyre had been suspended from a beam at head height and was intended to hit anyone entering in the face. Fortunately the first firefighter it hit in the face was wearing his breathing apparatus mask and wasn't injured.

One funny incident I remember with regards to injections and syringes was when the fire brigade decided that they would offer free Tetanus jabs to any firefighter who wanted to take them up. I thought it was a good idea as you were often at risk of cuts from glass or wire.

I had an injection in my arm and within 24 hours my arm blew up like a balloon. When I went to see my GP and told him I had received a Tetanus jab on a fire station he wasn't very happy and suggested fire stations were not very sterile places to provide injections.

Another firefighter had the Tetanus jab and a couple of nights later while on duty in the mess he sliced his hand opening a tin of corn beef. He was taken to the local A&E department for stitches and then the sister in charge told him to drop his trousers for a Tetanus jab.

The firefighter smiled and said it was okay as he had a Tetanus jab about a month ago. The Sister said, "Are you going to drop your trousers or do I have to pull them off you? You are not leaving here without a Tetanus jab."

A rush construction job gone wrong

One very unusual rescue I was involved with concerned a workman trapped in a trench. I was at home at lunchtime when my pager went off and informed me of the incident.

Living only five minutes away, I quickly arrived at the address to find a building site with a trench at least three metres *(almost 10 feet)* deep. Straddling the trench was a large mechanical digger. The weight of the machine was causing the sides of the trench to crumble slowly.

Lying in the trench under a pile of bricks was a workman. Removing the bricks off the man were a firefighter and a paramedic. As well as having the sides starting to crumble, the trench was slowly filling up with water.

The Station Officer said he wanted to withdraw the firefighter and the paramedic because the trench could collapse at any time and all three of them would be buried under tonnes of soil.

I had always prided myself on the need to save life at all costs and that included my firefighter and the paramedic. But, after making a cautious assessment, I was not prepared to take an extreme risk.

I asked the paramedic how serious the man's injuries were. The response was that he had crush injuries and, if he was not rescued quickly, would lose his leg and possibly his life.

I ordered the remainder of the firefighters around the trench to bring two ropes from the fire appliance and a scoop stretcher from the Emergency Tender, which was also in attendance.

I instructed the fire fighter in the trench to tie a line around his waist and then tie one around the paramedic's waist. I explained that we would lower a scoop stretcher into the trench. They were to get the casualty into the scoop stretcher as quickly as possible, and then we would pull all three out of the trench.

The remainder of the crew was ordered to stand well back from the edges of the trench and pull when the order was given. The casualty screamed loudly as he was grabbed and thrown into the stretcher. He was quickly secured, and pulled up the sides of the trench, followed immediately by the paramedic and the firefighter.

I had taken a serious risk in committing people into the trench. The Health & Safety Executive arrived shortly after the emergency services left and issued a Prohibition Notice, effectively closing the site for a number of weeks to investigate the accident.

In my report to senior management I recommended commendations for both the firefighter and the paramedic. My recommendation was duly accepted and a few months later I was at the ceremony when commendations were presented to both men.

The firefighter had experience of building sites and told me that when he jumped down into the trench he spoke to the casualty and asked him what the hell he was doing there while the machine was digging out the foundations. The man had replied that it was a rush job.

The firefighter told him he would get the sack when the foreman found out. The casualty replied that the foreman was his dad and he was the one who had told him to direct the digger from inside the trench.

The paramedic thanked me at the awards ceremony for the recommendation and asked why I had tied a rope around him as well as the firefighter.

I said that once I took charge of the rescue, his life was also my responsibility, just as the life of the casualty was his.

Fire arms at the incident scene

On a number of occasions during my time in Toxteth as a Station Officer the station responded to incidents that involved firearms. The first one I attended was a few days before the Pope's visit to Liverpool in 1982.

I had responded as part of the first attendance to the smell of burning in Gambia Terrace, which overlooks the Anglican Cathedral.

Gambia Terrace at the time contained many poorly built apartments within once grand houses. As there was no obvious sign of smoke or flames but a definite smell of burning, the fire crews had to knock on every door systematically. If no one answered the door, it was a case of lifting the letterbox and checking visually for signs of smoke or sniffing for smoke.

Eventually we arrived at the source of the burning smell. The occupier did not open the door, so we had to force entry into the flat. The cause of the alarm was a pan of cooking left on the stove.

Two firefighters entered the flat in breathing apparatus to check if anyone had been overcome by smoke, to extinguish the fire and to ventilate the property. One of them came out of the flat and beckoned me over. Taking off his mask, he told me there was a rifle on the couch in the back room.

I know I have watched too many films but when I went into the room I thought the window gave a perfect location for a sniper to take a shot at anyone visiting the Cathedral. Such a visitor would shortly be the Pope, so I requested Fire Control to contact the police and ask them to attend.

The normal response when Fire Brigade Control contacted Police Control was for the police to ask what was the reason for requesting their attendance.

Although they shouldn't, lots of people listen to the emergency services radio transmissions. I therefore didn't want to state that there was a firearm in one of the apartments, so I said we had found a weapon.

Back came the question: "What sort of weapon?"

Realising that this could end up as '20 Questions', but not wanting to state the full nature of the situation on the open airways, I responded: "A firearm".

Back came another question: "What sort of firearm?" Having at this point lost the will to carry on, I replied testily: "A big one". Several police cars arrived within three minutes and I left it with them.

The second time I attended such an incident occurred just after we had come on duty on a Friday night. We responded to a car on fire about two minutes away from the station in Princes Road, one of the main connecting roads of the area. As it was dark, we could see the flames from the vehicle behind one of the houses.

We arrived to find a sporty Ford vehicle blazing away. Normal procedure again was to call Control to ask for the police to attend and give the reason as 'Suspected stolen vehicle'. As usual for a Friday night in Toxteth, Control responded that the police were unable to attend due to operational commitments.

At this point one of my crew came over and said that just before we turned out he was watching the local news on the BBC television channel. There had been reports of an armed robbery committed by a number of men who had driven off in a Ford vehicle, and if anyone had seen the vehicle could they contact the police.

So, back on the radio to Control. I asked if they would inform the police that this may a vehicle of interest to them. Within five minutes the police helicopter was directly overhead, shining a very powerful light onto the scene. This light is so bright it tends to disorientate you if you are directly underneath.

Soon the scene was swarming with police cars. The senior police officer asked if we had searched the vehicle and had we found a gun? I replied that as the vehicle had been set alight with what I suspected to be petrol, we had only just extinguished the fire. Scene-of-Crime officers took over and we returned to the station.

The most unpleasant experience happened to one of the other Watches, called by the police to assist in locating a weapon that a gunman had dropped on a roof while being pursued.

The turntable ladder was required as the roof was more than 20 metres *(60.6 feet)* high. Two firemen went up on the roof after escorting police officers up the ladder. One of the officers shouted that he had found a gun when a ground-based searchlight illuminated the rooftop.

One of the firefighters lived with his mother in the Toxteth area and someone in the crowd watching below must have recognised him. A couple of days later, the windows in his mother's house were smashed as a punishment for assisting the police.

Eventually he and his mother had to move out of the district to avoid any further retaliation.

CHAPTER FIFTEEN

Training in fighting ship fires

In 1996 I had to attend a three-week Ship Firefighting Course at the Fire Service College at Moreton-in-Marsh, in Gloucestershire.

The courses were very intensive. They had amazing facilities on the site, and areas away from the college were also used during the training.

The reason we had to attend the course was due to Liverpool being a major port. If a ship heading for Liverpool caught fire, fire crews would have to be airlifted out to the vessel to assist with firefighting on board.

In the grounds of Fire Service College they had built a large concrete ship, surrounded by water. This could be used for simulating a ship fire at sea as well as in dock.

One of the exercises we took part in involved the assistance of a Royal Navy helicopter. It would land in the college grounds and the officers on the course would load equipment onto it. The helicopter would then fly around the college for a few minutes before all the officers on board were winched down onto the ship.

As we finished loading the helicopter on one exercise, one of the Royal Navy crew asked me to fetch a set of bolt-cutters from one of the many fire engines that were lined up by the ship.

I asked why they needed bolt-cutters and was told that, if the helicopter got into difficulty when they were lowering one of us by winch, they would cut through the winch cable to avoid the rotor blades becoming tangled: Navy humour.

When the helicopter was loaded, the Royal Navy guys used to put on a bit of an act when they were flying us to the ship. They would bank sharply left and right throwing us about inside. By the time it was your turn to be winched down you were glad to be re-united with your stomach and lowered onto the ship.

Once on the ship of course it was on fire and very hot.

I had experience of a number of ship fires in Liverpool and they are most unpleasant, due to the heat being contained by the metal structure of the vessel and the difficulty of getting charge hose lines down the passageways or into the engine room.

We were split into teams of four on one exercise. I was with an Officer from Bermuda, two Scots, one from the Highlands and Islands Fire Service and a guy from Grampian Fire Brigade.

Sometimes during exercises it was best to keep your mouth shut, do the job that was required, and sit through a de-brief. At the end everyone would be criticised by the college staff for something they did or didn't do. This particular day, one of the team was put in charge and we had to follow his instructions.

We made our way onto the lower decks of the ship where it was extremely hot. We had pulled a charge length of hose with us, and when we reached the passenger cabins it was obvious that the fire was coming from the deck below. The intense heat was rising upwards.

The guy in charge stopped us and said that he was going to go alone down a staircase on to the deck below to see if he could locate the seat of the fire.

When he asked if we had any questions, I enquired whether he could give me the names of his next of kin. He looked puzzled.

I said: "If you go down that staircase without any water you will be roasted alive." He made a tactical decision, changed his mind and said we should search the cabins on the floor we were currently on.

The officer from Bermuda and I entered the first cabin, found a dummy casualty and quickly made our way back up to the main deck. There we sank to the floor, removed our breathing apparatus and drank copious quantities of water.

Some time later during the exercise, an officer from Kent Fire Brigade collapsed due to heat exhaustion. He had to be brought up from the lower decks, lifted off the ship by hydraulic platform and taken by ambulance to the nearest hospital.

Kent Fire Brigade was at that time undertaking trials of an all-in-one fire suit that did away with a separate fire tunic and drip pants. It appeared that the officer had become dehydrated and suffered from heat exhaustion because of the intense heat inside the suit.

It was good training at the college because it was not theoretical but very much replicated incidents you may come across during your career.

A week or so after the helicopter exercise we were taken to Cotswold Country Park, accompanied by a hydraulic platform. The exercise was to simulate jumping into the water from the deck of a vessel at sea and making your way to a life raft in the park lake.

A pal of mine had attended this course a few months previously and gave me this advice: whatever you do, don't jump into the water early on. If you do you'll be in the cold water or shivering wet in the life raft for a long time.

The hydraulic platform was extended to 50 feet above the water and we climbed up to the platform in groups of four. We all wore life jackets and were told that when we jumped to keep our heads up and hold the life jacket across the chest so that it didn't hurt our neck when we hit the water.

I positioned myself near the back of the queue along with one of my fellow officers from Merseyside. We watched as guys came down from the platform, hit the water, disappeared, bobbed back up to the surface, swam to the life raft, and climbed aboard.

Eventually, there were just two of us on the platform - the last to jump. My fellow Merseyside officer had doubts now about whether he could jump from such a height into the water. I tried to convince him it wasn't a problem and said I would be right behind him.

Eventually he jumped and I made the mistake of watching him all the way down. "Wow. That looks such a long way," I thought.

"Too late now" I realised, and stepped out into space. I plunged down into the water like a stone and my feet touched the bottom of the lake before I came up at a rate of knots to the surface. I swam to the life raft and climbed aboard.

"Glad that's over," I thought.

However, one of the bright sparks on the course piped up and suggested: "Why don't they take the platform up to 70 feet?" He was quickly silenced, and we returned to the college, having completed another exercise.

The officers in charge of the training courses were normally on secondment from their own brigade, and were at least one rank above the rank at the college. Sometimes their lack of experience in many areas of firefighting and leadership was exposed.

During exercises, various members of the course were designated to follow and log the procedures taken by the officers put in charge of each exercise. I was designated to follow an officer from West Midlands Fire Brigade who turned out to a mock traffic accident on the road section of the college airfield.

When the officer arrived, he found a bus had collided with a lamppost and two dummy casualties were wedged under seats on the top deck of the bus.

The officer quickly gave his instructions to his crew of four firefighters to remove the bolts holding the seats to the floor of the top deck. As the bus was an old model with a small spiral type staircase, he decided to strap the dummies onto ladder sections and take them out through the emergency exit at the rear of the top deck.

To ensure a smooth transition, he ordered the driver to reverse the fire engine until it was directly under the emergency exit.

The two casualties were smoothly released, very carefully passed out through the emergency exit and lowered to the ground floor, where an ambulance took them away.

The exercise debrief was overseen by a young-looking Divisional Officer who asked for my report on the actions of the officer in charge.

I stated that I thought that he was cool in carrying out his initial assessment; quick to decide his course of action to complete the rescue; and his use of the rear window in the bus to reduce the risk of further injury to the casualties by attempting to take them down the staircase was excellent.

The response I got from the Divisional Officer left me speechless. Bear in mind that at the time all the course were sitting on the lower deck of the bus for the debrief. He stood up and said the officer in charge got too involved. He should have delegated, got off the bus and stood and watched.

I burst out laughing. This didn't go down well.

He continued that, in his opinion, a good Officer in Charge at an incident would stand with feet shoulder-width apart, with his hands clasped loosely behind his back and gently rock backwards and forwards, thinking beautiful thoughts.

I had had enough of this now.

"Excuse me, sir," I said. "If I were standing at an incident in Liverpool with my hands behind my back rocking backwards and forwards – and the Chief Fire Officer strode up and said, "What are you doing, Fanning?" and I replied, "Having beautiful thoughts, sir" – I would be put in the nearest ambulance and driven to the funny farm.

The whole course collapsed into laughter.

Some years later I returned on another course as I had had a second promotion and needed to attend the next phase. As part of this course we had to spend three days in the Breathing Apparatus Section at the College.

On day one we were put through a hard physical exercise in 100% humidity conditions wearing breathing apparatus and carrying heavy drums full of sand up and over various objects. At various stages during the exercise one of the instructors would shout, "Are you okay?" and stick a thermometer in the side of your face mask to check the temperature.

One by one guys started to fall down with physical exhaustion during the exercise. After about 20 minutes I gave up and was taken outside.

We were left to recover and not checked to see if anyone was really distressed.

The following day before the next exercise a couple of guys on the course raised their concerns with the Breathing Apparatus Section's senior officer. He simply waved them away.

As part of the next exercise I was in a team of two that followed a length of hose down a staircase into a very hot room.

When you wear a breathing apparatus mask your ears are exposed and they are the best indicators of when it is really hot, and this room was roasting.

Our task was to knock the fire down and make our way into a lower section and recover any dummy casualties we found. My companion and I lay on the floor and dragged the hose towards us so we could put a spray on the fire and cool it down sufficiently to pass and reach the lower section. However, the hose wasn't charged with water so we had to withdraw rapidly just as our air started to run out.

At the debrief the course raised questions as to why the temperature was in excess of 1,000°C and the water supply had been shut off. We suspected this was because of the issues raised after the first exercise.

The Senior Officer in charge stood up and stated that he was quite prepared for someone to die during an exercise in his Breathing Apparatus Complex. At this, a number of the course stood up and walked out. I said that if someone died in his complex he would have to stand in the witness box at the Coroner's Inquest Hearing, in front of the television reporters, the radio and print press and the dead firefighter's relatives, and repeat that statement and see what the jury and the coroner made of his remarks.

It was absolute madness.

The following week we arrived at the Royal Naval College at Portsmouth where were treated to the delights of a ship simulator after it has been hit by a missile and starts to take on water very quickly. Once again I had been pre-warned about this exercise and the advice was to try not to end up on the lower decks because they fill up with water the quickest.

Imagine my delight when the Royal Naval guy dishing out the tasks asked if there were any Scousers on the course *('Scouser' is a colloquial term for people from Liverpool)*. Well, there were four of us. We were duly designated as the pump crew and would have to pump the water out of the vessel after the missile hit, to allow the guys on the lower decks to plug the holes in the vessel with wood and other pieces of equipment to hand.

Thinking this was good news, we waited on one of the upper decks with lengths of hose to attach to a hydrant we had spotted on the main deck.

The simulator's loudspeaker system made an announcement warning the crew that there were missiles inbound. Suddenly there was a loud bang, the lights went out and the simulator began to rock up and down making movements that made walking in a straight line extremely difficult.

The Royal Navy guy who had seemed to like Scousers shouted to the pump crew to get up on deck and connect hose to the hydrant. I climbed a metal ladder and, as I began to undo the hatch cover, water started to trickle in. I couldn't understand why, when I finally opened the hatch fully, I got absolutely soaked and so did the rest of my crew.

The Royal Navy guys had sabotaged the deck hydrant, saying it had been hit by shrapnel and so we could not use it. By the time we had located another hydrant and a working pump the guys on the lower decks were up to their necks in water and screaming to us to 'get the bloody water out'.

Ten minutes or so later we were making a good fist of it but needed more hose. One of the Royal Navy guys gave us two more lengths of hose to use. Making our way back up on deck we connected the additional hose only to discover that we had been given burst lengths of hose to slow down our attempts in overcoming the level of water.

Eventually we had removed sufficient water to enable many holes to be sealed and for our course colleagues to breathe a bit easier. It was only at this point I suddenly felt sea sick because of the violent motion of the simulator. Fortunately, the exercise was terminated shortly afterwards.

After we had showered, we changed into our undress uniforms and went into the officer's mess where we were waited upon by Royal Navy junior officers: the food was excellent. After the meal we adjourned to the bar where I ordered for my colleagues and myself: two whiskies and two brandies.

The bar steward asked me for one pound in payment. I looked at him in surprise and suggested he had made a mistake and forgot to charge for all the drinks. He replied in the negative and explained that it was only 25 pence a shot. So I decided that I would stay in the bar while many of the other guys went out to taste the night life in Portsmouth.

It was an amazing three weeks and I enjoyed it enormously. I left confident that if the need ever arose to tackle another ship on fire in the future, what I had learnt would definitely assist me.

CHAPTER SIXTEEN

Outreach to young people in the community

As I said in an earlier tale, I had joined the Toxteth Crime Prevention Panel. After 12 months or so of attending meetings as a Board Member, I was invited to become Chairman, and accepted.

We had to raise funds for initiatives to keep young people occupied and, hopefully, away from a path of crime. It was decided to hold a fundraising event at the Holiday Inn in Liverpool city centre and invite people from community groups to attend.

I approached an ex-fireman, Paul Martin, to perform at the event. Paul was now a local comedian working under the stage name of 'Willie Miller'. He was great at organising such functions and suggested a local singing group we could ask to appear. Then we went to the hotel to sort out catering and the timetable for the event.

Paul took charge of everything. He even suggested to the hotel management that, as the Crime Prevention Panel were bringing in lots of people to the event, they should provide raffle prizes and two rooms of accommodation – one for himself and one for my wife and me.

The event was a great success and well attended by lots of community groups. We raised more than £4,000 towards the needed funds. When we turned up at our next Panel meeting, the Police said that the money should fund schemes for youngsters in the community who were constantly in trouble and on the verge of prison sentences.

I did not agree and neither did a number of Panel members.

What message does that send out to youngsters in the local community who behave themselves and do not cause trouble?

There was a heated debate and eventually the money was split between two causes, one for young offenders and the other for community groups such as youth clubs.

I enjoyed working on the Panel but after two years the then Chief Constable decided to disband local Crime Prevention Panels, without any valid reason – or so it seemed.

More strike action

I was beginning to look at when I might retire from the Fire Service as I was approaching 50. Although I was still enjoying the role as Station Commander, the constant disturbance during the early hours of the morning was beginning to lose its attraction.

Strike action was taking place once again but only locally. The Fire Brigades Union decided to call one-day strikes when the Local Authority decided to take some leave entitlement away from the men and women on the stations.

I honestly thought there were better reasons to strike over, such as the threat to close a number of stations, a cause where I felt we would have received a lot more public support.

The problem for me as the Station Commander was that I had to lock and secure the station when the strike began and then unlock it before the Watches were due to return to duty after the strike period.

One morning after strike action the night before, I was having a cup of tea at home before opening up the station at 9am and listening to the local radio.

The news headline was that a man had died in a fire in a flat during the strike action. I whispered a silent prayer hoping that it had not been in my station area. Unfortunately it was.

When I arrived at the Fire Station at 8.30 am, television cameras and reporters were camped out opposite. I unlocked the station gate and drove my car in, before re-locking the entrance. The telephone was ringing as I entered the station office. I picked up the receiver and a voice asked for the Station Commander, I replied that I was the Commander. The caller was a reporter and he asked how I felt about causing the death of a man by going on strike the night before.

The calls came thick and fast that morning, and all I could do was refer the callers to the local Fire Brigades Union representative, as they had decided the strike dates.

I decided not long after this series of strikes that I would do one more year and retire in 1999 at the age of 51.

Cotton candy on fire

It wasn't a quiet year and unfortunately there were four fatalities in fires alone, as well as a couple of people found dead in properties after the crews had been called out to gain entry. The last large fire I attended was a call to an ice-cream manufacturer in Jamaica Street.

I had been turned out to a fire on the Wirral on the other side of the River Mersey, and had reached the Albert Dock when I was turned back after receiving an update that the fire did not require my attendance.

As I drove back towards home, on the car radio I heard the pump from Toxteth turn out to a factory in an industrial area just off the city centre.

The first appliance that arrived had sent an assistance message for two additional pumps. With that message I knew I would have to attend and, being so close, I arrived before the two additional pumps.

It was about 18.30 and the factory was locked up, but there was a serious fire breaking through the roof on one side of the building. The roof construction was asbestos sheeting and this was exploding with the heat of the fire which was spreading very quickly.

I decided to make the attendance up to eight pumps.

We would need to gain access to the factory and there would have to be many firefighters in breathing apparatus – not just for the smoke from the fire, but as protection from the asbestos particles that were showering down around the building.

Three very experienced station officers had arrived and were awaiting instructions. This was a bonus because I knew I could allocate an area of the incident to each of them, leave them to carry out my instructions and report back to me if they required any further assistance. The firefighting went like clockwork and the blaze was brought under control within two hours with no injuries. A large part of the building saved from fire damage.

The following day the fire investigation team found that the cause of the fire had been a drum of lolly-ice liquid that had been left too close to a heater inside the factory.

The liquid in concentrated form was extremely flammable and the drum may have had a small leak. The vapours from the liquid would have ignited readily with heat from the heater.

The factory did not open again. The building was later demolished and the site lay vacant for many years.

Avoidable domestic fires

A number of the fatalities in my last year were caused by medical conditions, with the fire being either an after-effect or the cause of a medical condition worsening.

One fatality was totally avoidable but mirrored a number of similar deaths through the same cause during my 35 years in the fire service.

The preventable fatality was only discovered about 18 hours after the fire started. It was a Sunday night and the Control Room received a call from a tenant in one of the roads in Anfield near to Liverpool Football Club's football ground. The caller stated that the smoke alarm next door had been beeping all day and there was no reply when they had knocked on the door.

The appliances from West Derby Road were mobilised and when they forced entry, the occupier was found dead on the couch in the living room. The cause of the fire was a chip pan that the male occupier had lit after coming home from the pub after a night's drinking. While waiting for the chips to cook, the occupier had lain down on the couch and fallen asleep. Having inhaled the smoke from the blaze, he never woke up.

For many years chip pans have caused thousands of fires across the country and resulted in numerous deaths. In recognition of this there was a move to remove the risk of chip-pan fires by encouraging cooking oven chips, but there were still too many people who were prepared to take the risk, especially after consuming a lot of alcohol.

Firefighters' Attitude Improvement Meeting

On every team there are times when some of the members are carrying more than their fair share of the load and the team needs a bit of a jolt. There came a time for one of my teams when a jolt certainly was due. This was my method.

On a training session, I told my Toxteth firefighters that someone who lived in Toxteth had won many millions on the lottery and wanted to start a new football team to rival Everton and Liverpool. He was going to call the team Toxteth United. So I asked them what he would need to have a successful team.

Football is the 'lingua franca' of Liverpool. You can give all sorts of examples but people instantly get any that are football focused. The group perked up and seemed interested. Back came the answers: a manager, a coach, a team, a pitch, kit, the right equipment, and fans.

I drew a football pitch on the white board and put in a set of goal posts:

> *In goal* I put myself, the Station Officer.
> *The fullbacks* were my other two ranks.
> *The midfield* were the four drivers on the watch.
> *The forward line* was made up from any four from the six firemen on the watch.

There were puzzled looks. "What's this team?"

I responded like this:

> Well, I am in goal because *the goalkeeper* has to stop anything getting past him. It's just the same for the Station Officer: he doesn't want anything getting past him up the line to Division.
>
> The goalkeeper is also *the manager*: he supervises the team; he makes sure they play by the rules for health and safety; he makes sure that he never puts them in danger.

He is also *the coach*. That's why we have to practice drills so that when we play a game *(fire or traffic accident)* we don't lose anyone - and that includes the public.

The two full backs have to support the goalkeeper in everything he does. They have to follow the game plan, especially when the goalkeeper is on holiday or on a training course. They don't suddenly relax and lose the game pattern.

The drivers have to drive the team to the correct place on the pitch *(the station area)*. This caused some embarrassment because when I first arrived, on a couple of occasions when we turned out, the driver told me he didn't know where a particular road was. This meant I had to learn the station area within the first week I arrived. Any driver who said he wasn't sure or didn't know the route was stood down until he could direct me verbally to ten roads in the area.

What about *the firefighters*? Well they were the ones who scored the goals or got the plaudits for the team. They were the ones who rescued the fans *(members of the public)* from danger.

If they were late for the game *(duty)* we were a man down and it may affect our performance and we may let the fans down.

It was important that they wore the correct kit and their kit was clean so the fans were impressed by their local team *(I had noticed that many times their uniforms were filthy)*.

I then went on again about my role as the manager.

Every time the fire alarm goes I had to respond. The drivers and the firemen would alternate on different shifts, but I was always in the front.

When the fire engine returned to the station, they would wash up and then sit watching the TV or play pool or cards. I would start to write the fire report that may take an hour or so, depending on the particular game we had just attended.

I was responsible for their kit, every chair they sat on and table they sat at, every knife fork and spoon they used.

I put my salary figure next to the goal posts and asked the question: with all that responsibility, was I giving value for money.

I did the same for the ranks, drivers and firefighters and asked the same question. Was the team getting value for money from every player?

The team had some of the worse sickness records in the division. When the good team players wanted a rest they couldn't get a game off because the sick players had left the team very short.

My closing statement was that in this team I was the most important player because if anything got past me then the team and I would suffer and we may end up being relegated to other teams *(stations)* in the division.

It really did work. Some of the habitual sickies bucked their ideas up and a couple of the watch said that I wasn't getting enough money for the job I was doing.

Football may not be the language your team understands, but find what is and make everyone understand the roles, responsibilities and challenges of each player.

Drawing the final line

The fire brigade was changing now. There was talk of firefighters having to achieve an NVQ in putting up ladders.

A National Vocational Certificate could be taught in a college – often by those who had learned the theory, but not the practice, so students would emerge thinking they knew what to do from a theoretical exercise rather than the real experience.

In my opinion standards were about to drop and I was not prepared to be a part of it.

I decided that I would leave Merseyside Fire Brigade in May 1999 after 35 very happy years during which I had enjoyed every day and every night of my career.

I had seen acts of amazing bravery and courage which at times I couldn't believe I was watching.

There were dedicated firefighters on all the Watches on all the stations I served on, and eventually had the honour to command.

When we arrived at any incident – a fire, road traffic accident or a flooding – I knew that when I gave out the instructions to my crew they would carry it out exactly as I had told them. I knew that they realised that I would never put their lives in danger while they were under my leadership.

My career had started very slowly at Mather Avenue Fire Station, which is now closed: it went even slower at Banks Road, also closed, and drifted along at Belle Vale. But once I moved through the ranks, it began to race along.

Toxteth was my dream posting and, looking back, had I been posted there straight from my Junior Fireman days, I might well have remained a fireman throughout my entire career, enjoying the total firefighting role.

In fact, the way my career went over the years probably made me a better and more experienced officer.

Because of my own experience, I knew what it was like for the guys on quiet stations with the constant boredom, and also the effect of the constant turnouts on the firefighters at the busier stations.

Firefighters of my era never received any counselling after attending a fatal fire or traffic accident.

This maybe one of the reasons that after starting their retirement some of my former colleagues turned to drink, suffered from depression, and even committed suicide.

My advice to anyone entering the fire service anywhere in the world today would be that you cannot buy experience.

You gain experience through the incidents you attend. Learn from both good and bad practices, good and bad managers.

As you rise through the ranks put into practice everything you have learnt to good use.

Finally, always expect the unexpected.

As a firefighter you will never be disappointed.

Fanning the Flames

www.ingramcontent.com/pod-product-compliance
Lightning Source LLC
Chambersburg PA
CBHW072017070526
44583CB00015B/1512